the
Lean
and
Happy Home

Photograph by Anna Huerta

Eva Jarlsdotter worked for almost a decade in journalism before taking up leadership roles in communications, corporate social responsibility, and telecoms. She's now a writer, consultant, and lecturer. Eva holds a degree in Journalism and an executive MBA from the Stockholm School of Economics. She lives in Stockholm with her husband and their three children in an old house with an apple orchard.

the
Lean
and
Happy Home

EVA JARLSDOTTER

Translated by Amanda Larsson

First published in Great Britain in 2019 by Yellow Kite
An imprint of Hodder & Stoughton
An Hachette UK company

First self-published as *From Frustration to Flow with Lean at Home*

1

A CIP catalogue record for this title is available from the British Library

Hardback ISBN 978 1 529 33780 8
eBook ISBN 978 1 529 33929 1

Printed and bound in Great Britain by Clays Ltd, Elcograf S.p.A.

Hodder & Stoughton policy is to use papers that are natural, renewable
and recyclable products and made from wood grown in sustainable
forests. The logging and manufacturing processes are expected to
conform to the environmental regulations of the country of origin.

Yellow Kite
Hodder & Stoughton Ltd
Carmelite House
50 Victoria Embankment
London EC4Y 0DZ

www.yellowkitebooks.co.uk

*For Mattias, with whom I wrote this book, and for
Vendela, Tuva, and Samuel, who inspired us to write it.*

Table of Contents

PREFACE: FROM FRUSTRATION TO FLOW WITH LEAN

Does your home flow? Is it sustainable and harmonious? Do you and your partner share the same picture of what makes a good home, and do you keep watch over your finances, and what goes on in your children's lives? Do you appreciate and validate one another's ideas? Are you achieving your dreams? Does everyone in your home contribute to housework? Do you successfully meet each family member's needs, without friction or frustration?

If that is the case – you don't really need this book.

Our family faced major challenges in late spring 2011. For better or worse, I had finally decided to leave my Vice President role at a telecom company to finish the trilogy I had been writing for nearly a decade, a decision that would cut our income by more than half. Our home was loving, but chaotic. We had no control, and we were incredibly reactive. To prevent our inability to organize our daily lives from affecting our three kids (or anyone else), we became masters of improvisation. Our son had just started nursery, and his big sisters were in their last terms of nursery and reception. I was constantly exhausted, and every molehill felt like a Himalayan climb. We struggled to conquer daily life while watching so many others do everything in their power to escape.

Out of pure survival instinct, we began to implement lean at home. At first, it was unintentional, but a pattern eventually emerged, like interwoven threads forming figures in a tapestry. My husband, Mattias, and I had worked with lean in business and in healthcare. In late spring 2011, when things were at their most hectic, we began to systematically use the tools and philosophy at home. After only nine months – although the journey had just begun – we noticed astronomical, astounding results.

Lean has been spreading across the world like wildfire ever since the early twentieth century, when Sakichi Toyoda of Japan began establishing Toyota Industries and developing lean philosophy. Lean has marched triumphantly from Toyota and the car industry to hospitals, prosecution offices and service companies. But it has not yet been applied to the home.

In the family and in the home, we are hard on one another's love, trust and self-esteem; we put a strain on the environment and on ourselves, and many people waste resources – both time and money.Lean curtails that wastefulness. Persistent work with lean can dramatically reduce waste and create a more sustainable, harmonious home – and ultimately, a more sustainable society.

A lean management consultant with an excellent reputation recently said that most leaders seem to focus on increasing productivity by 35–40% in the three to five years following the implementation of lean. He added that what they should really focus on is using lean to increase productivity by 400% in ten years. The same is true of family life. Our closest relationships help us evolve as people, but they can also cause us to come to a standstill, to get stuck in established roles, or to give up what we really want from life. Lean helps us do the best we can and live our dreams. All that's required is love, intention, and perseverance. Do you have what it takes?

OVERVIEW: THE BOOK'S THEMES

Lean is about focusing on value-creation, smoothly running processes, and reducing waste. I am therefore obliged to make sure that every word in this book creates value, every sentence flows, and that I do not waste your time. The book takes a few hours to read, and afterwards, you will have a toolbox to start working with lean at home.

In Chapter 1, I begin by briefly explaining what our daily life looked like before we started systematically implementing lean. Chapters 2–4 tell the story of lean – what it is, and how I've translated it into lean at home.

The subsequent chapters delve into the various pillars of lean at home, and each one concludes with concrete tips to begin using that particular aspect of the philosophy. Chapter 5 addresses the heart of lean at home: going from a frustrating, bottleneck-filled life to days that run smoothly.

In Chapter 6, I explain how to begin your journey, and you will learn how to go from where you are now to where you want to be. I also discuss how to stop seeing problems as negatives but as opportunities in disguise, something to fine tune.

Chapter 7 focuses on how to use lean at home to reduce domestic waste. Although every household may have unique problems, the common denominator shared by most people – whether real or perceived – is a lack of time, money, and energy. Lean at home will help you to make the most of your resources and the resources of our planet, and will help you to find value in what you currently perceive to be waste.

Chapter 8 focuses on visual planning and creating predictability and expectation as you fit the pieces of your life together. It presents tools that will help you stop feeling like you're being chased, and teach you how to take full control of your life.

Chapter 9 is about systematically creating and maintaining organization. In our home, we've established a habit inspired by lean that is as sacred as a Sunday family dinner.

Chapter 10 is your chance for reflection. Look back to learn, and to make sure you've met basic needs, rather than wasting energy on compensatory ones. Look to the future, consider your goals and dreams, and determine how you will make them a reality.

Chapter 11 presents tools to create participation and equality. Here, you will learn how to make sure everyone contributes their abilities, and how to make sure no individual pulls the entire load alone, burdened with the task of "home project leader".

Chapter 12 paints a picture of the incredible results our family has achieved in just over a year with lean at home. If you are still hesitant to read this book, I think you should start there. After that, I hope you decide to invest a few hours reading the rest of the book.

In chapters 13 and 14, I offer practical tips for how to begin trying lean at home.

1

OUR HOUSE: CHAOTIC BUT LOVING

*– how we implemented lean
out of pure survival instinct*

In the late spring of 2011, our home was more chaotic than usual. Samuel had just started nursery, Tuva was in her last term of nursery, and Vendela was in reception. Our jobs were hyper-scheduled and enormously stressful. As a specialist in family practice at a medical center, Mattias had a new patient every fifteen minutes – fifteen vital minutes that required presence and precision. All day long, I attended a string of meetings as Vice President of an international telecom company, TeliaSonera, and the night shift began when the kids went to sleep at nine o'clock. TeliaSonera was about to launch a new brand for all wholly owned companies in the enterprise – from Nepal to Norway, from Kazakhstan to Lithuania, and I was one of the key players.

A glimpse of our reflections in the mirror at that time revealed a tired, middle-aged couple. Silver splashes appeared in Mattias' five o'clock shadow; white roots sprouted in my bleached blonde hair. The curiosity that once sparkled in our eyes had been replaced by sadness, a dull melancholy. Our muscles languished after years of neglecting to exercise.

Our home, a beautiful 1940s wooden house with a dazzling garden, should have been a place to rest, enjoy, socialize, and grow.

But it wasn't really.

The first bottleneck

We wanted an open, welcoming home, where setting an extra place for a friend was never a problem, but we rarely even knew what we were going to serve. Unlikely combinations characterized our improvised dinners for friends of all ages, whom we tried to escort into the house through our first bottleneck: the cluttered hallway.

After the meal, we threw away about one third of our food, on average, which is statistically typical for rich countries.

Many things came as a surprise: dinners, holidays, conferences, birthday parties, daycare planning days, business trips abroad. Usually, we managed to fudge it and improvise, and one set of grandparents or the other frequently came to the rescue.

Vital sphere

More than 20 piles of clothing decorated our home; in fact, our wardrobes were fairly empty, because our clothes were usually in the washing machine. Or slung over the bed frame. Or hanging from the stair railing, or rumpled on a desk chair, or stuffed into the enormous chest of garments waiting to be ironed...

We started buying storage systems at breakneck speed. One room was a dressing room, but it overflowed with clothing. We went online and bought a gorgeous old linen cupboard and a glazed bookcase; we set up shelf after shelf. Nothing helped. Our home was flooded.

We spent endless hours each week looking for things, and all too often we never found them – we just bought a duplicate, and, occasionally, even a triplicate. Our daily lives were not exactly enjoyable, and we knew how vital the home sphere is for children as they grow up. The thought gnawed at us. We felt that we were at a crossroads. In addition, I had decided to resign, in order to finally finish the trilogy I had been writing since our oldest daughter was born. Instead of working twelve hours a day, I would finally have an eight-hour day, like almost everyone else.

Eight years of intense work, countless trips, an executive MBA degree program and many sleepless nights had started taking their toll. I was tremendously worn out. Our self-esteem and confidence were wearing thin, and we were wasteful with everything: time, money, and the environment. We had to make a change.

Without realizing it at first, we began to implement lean in our home out of pure survival instinct.

2

IT STARTED IN JAPAN

*– how a poor weaver's son
became an industry king*

To understand how lean came to be, let's look back a few centuries, to the Empire of Japan.

It began with Sakichi Toyoda. He was born one February day in 1867, in the village of Kosai in northern Japan. His mother was a poor weaver, and his father was a carpenter. Weaving was an important industry at the time, and Japan's decision-makers focused on small businesses and encouraged cottage industries, which were typically small workshops or factories with a handful of employees, or commercial weavers working at home. When Toyoda was in his 20s, he started making manual looms that were cheaper and better than the ones that existed. He was concerned about the backbreaking work that his mother, grandmother, and other neighborhood women had to do. He developed an automatic wooden loom with a mechanism that stopped the loom when a thread broke, rather than continuing to weave with a mistake. Sakichi Toyoda is often referred to as the "king of Japanese inventors", and is considered the father of the Japanese industrial revolution. In 1926, he founded Toyota Industries. Initially, the company made looms, but began to manufacture cars in 1937.

The thread's beginning and end

The mechanism that made the loom stop when the yarn broke formed the foundation for the system later developed and used in Toyota's car factories worldwide: the Toyota Production System (TPS). The system optimizes production by avoiding errors from the start – and tending to them immediately they occur.

When Sakichi Toyoda left his company to his son Kiichiro, he said,

> *"Everyone should take on a major project at least once in their lives. I spent most of my life inventing new kinds of looms. Now it's your turn. You should try to accomplish something that benefits society."*

Kiichiro Toyoda built up Toyota Motor Company according to his father's philosophy and leadership, but made improvements. He started from his father's weaving inventions, and saw symbolic threads running through the entire production. I think this thread metaphor is helpful. If you can recognize the processes, or streams, that run through an organization or a home, they are easier to understand. Lean is about keeping an eye on every stream, and understanding what truly creates value, and what is pure waste. It's about untangling all the knots to create smooth and easy processes. It's about seeing the beginning and the end of the thread, rather than a messy, matted ball of yarn that you can't bear the thought of beginning to untangle.

The end of waste

Post-war Japan was characterized by a shortage of most things. So, Toyoda focused on using resources properly and eliminating all types of waste. He built a sustainable organization long before sustainable development existed as a theory.

Kiichiro Toyoda said,

> *"All we do is watch how much time passes from the moment a customer gives us an order, to the moment we are paid. We shorten that time by eliminating anything that does not add value."*

Remember the thread metaphor. The start of the thread is when the customer submits an order, and the end is when Toyota receives payment. Anything that does not create value in between is eliminated. So, key concepts to keep in mind are: do things correctly, remove all waste, and focus on what is valuable, creates value, and can be fine tuned. What would your home look like if you thought about organizing it in terms of these key concepts? Or consider the reverse: if your workplace were organized like your home, what would your workplace be like? Would you tolerate such a workplace? Would you tolerate that kind of leadership?

At home, you or you and your partner are in charge. Do not shirk this responsibility by trying to escape.

The fact that all employees work with steady improvements makes lean a world-class and phenomenally powerful tool for change. It is a catalyst to create a culture of steady improvements and genuine learning. Imagine if you and your family worked with steady improvements and a culture of genuine learning. It would be hard to be stagnant.

When management consultants from the US tried to analyse and understand the success behind the Toyota Production System, they renamed it lean. Since then, the philosophy and methods have spread across the world like wildfire. The car industry, the rest of the manufacturing industry, service companies, and the public sector use lean.

But one kind of organization remains untouched: the home.

I have tried to pick up Sakichi Toyoda's baton when it comes to the idea that, at least once in your life, you should take on a huge project that benefits society. Sakichi Toyoda started by simplifying the backbreaking work his mother and other women performed at home with a loom, and then the philosophy was industrialized. In a way, I think the circle is complete when we see how we can reuse lean, bringing it from the industrial setting to the home, with lean at home.

3

WHAT IS LEAN?

– stream efficiency (and how it can make cancer care 500 times more efficient)

Maybe you've already worked with lean. If not, I'll try to sum up the philosophy and its most essential concepts in this chapter. The first time I encountered lean was at AstraZeneca's respiratory pharmaceuticals plant in Södertälje, near Stockholm, Sweden. It was 2004, and factory management had been inspired by vehicle manufacturer Scania in the same city, who had in turn been inspired by Toyota. It was powerful to see the operators' pride as they talked about 100% productivity increases, their steady work with continuous improvements, and their total control of successful deliveries to various markets worldwide. The results spread by word of mouth, and although the movement was grassroots, it was certainly with management's blessing. I organized a meeting in Södertälje, and we invited all of Group management from London to come and talk with representatives from all parts of AstraZeneca's Swedish operation, which had started implementing lean. They included the quality, finance, research, and communications departments, as well as other factories and support units. Listening to colleagues from various levels explain to management how lean had changed and improved the operation was magical.

Fujio Cho, President of Toyota Motor Corporation, has said that the operators on the floor do the truly value-adding work. That meeting made it incredibly clear that indeed, the power of change comes from the people on the floor, the people who understand the reality of what takes place. It was a cultural shift.

Some people liken lean to an operational strategy: it provides support for how to lead and run an organization.

Focus on streams

What are AstraZeneca and other organizations, such as the health-care system, doing? One essential basic action is to review the streams, or processes, that exist in the organization. In a nutshell, the following story of two women who live in different areas shows what that rather dry term, "stream efficiency," means in action. This real-life example is from the book *This is Lean* (by Niklas Modig and Par Åhlström). Jennifer and Cynthia each discover a lump in one breast. Jennifer will receive care 500 times faster than Cynthia. From her first visit to the nurse, to receiving a diagnosis, it takes two hours. Cynthia undergoes the same course of events, but the time between her first trip to the medical center and receiving a diagnosis is nearly 42 days. In other words: it takes two hours for one woman who has found a lump in her breast to be diagnosed, and it takes another woman 1,008 hours.

Jennifer had the good fortune of living in a city in which the university hospital had implemented lean, and launched a One-stop Breast Clinic. The multi-skilled team included a secretary, radiologist, pathologist, radiology nurse, assistant nurse, and a breast surgeon – all under one roof. This stream let Jennifer receive a diagnosis the same day she walked through the doctor's office doors. The thread from seeking treatment to diagnosis was straight and short.

In Cynthia's case, each nurse, doctor and surgeon certainly worked as efficiently as they could. The difference was in the organization of care, and the design of the course of treatment: the stream. The thread was tangled, knotted, broken. The difference was 41 days and 22 hours. 1,008 hours is plenty of time for a malignant tumor to penetrate deep into tissue. In addition to anxiety and a decreased chance of removing the cancer, such inefficient streams also cause a lot of extra work – phone calls to schedule the next visit, checking to see if a referral has arrived, scheduling another X-ray, and so on.

This is stream efficiency. And it can be a matter of life and death.

The pillars of lean

Lean has a number of pillars that I will introduce here. In the coming chapters, I'll translate them into lean at home.

1. **STREAM:** everything that happens from the moment a need arises to the time it is satisfied, for example: from a customer ordering a new car, to the car's delivery and the receipt of payment. Reviewing streams allows us to see what creates value and what is wasteful. You can see where bottlenecks and frustration arise, and create the conditions for processes to run smoothly. Think of clothing chain Zara, which has an incredibly short lead-time from a designer's first sketch to a finished dress hitting a store near you. Or consider the previous example: a woman with a suspicious lump in her breast who is in need of a diagnosis. Streams are all around us, overt or otherwise. You just need to learn to see them.

2. *KAIZEN:* continuous improvements. *Kaizen* can be summed up in five steps: (i) analyse the current situation, (ii) determine the desired future, (iii) decide what needs to be done, (iv) establish new procedures that make it easy to do things right, and (v) begin and follow up. *Kaizen* catalyses change in the streams that most need it. It creates a culture of continuous improvements and, according to the Toyota Way, should be run by whoever works directly with problems rather than by someone far removed from the value-creating work. This is where some top-down organizations make the cardinal mistake of bringing in "outside experts" with solutions, rather than listening to the real experts and their collected experience from the floor.

3. *MUDA:* Japanese for "waste". In lean, you steadily work to reduce all types of waste – everything from time and money to ingredients and the environment. According to lean, overproduction and lack of participation are two of the most common causes of waste. One way to work on reducing waste is to ask yourself "why" five times, which is called *Hadome*. This process can help you figure out the root cause of waste, not just the symptoms. Let's say you find a pool of oil on your factory floor, you could ask yourself the following questions: 1. Why is it there? A machine is leaking. 2. Why is the machine leaking? Because a gasket is defective. 3. Why is the gasket defective? Because it was not sufficiently durable. 4. Why wasn't the gasket durable? Because price was more important than quality to the purchasing department. 5. Why was price more important? Because the purchasing policy emphasized price over quality. In five questions, we've found the root cause of the problem, and now we can do something to fix it.

4. **KANBAN:** Japanese for "sign", *Kanban* is a visual planning board providing a complete overview of everything that goes on in the factory, at the hospital, or in the information department. Usually taking less than fifteen minutes, *Kanban* meetings are so-called stand-up meetings, where each team member gives a rundown of their current status and plans. Afterwards, everyone knows precisely what needs to be done. The meetings make employees more proactive, create a sense of participation, and give participants the opportunity to have an influence. The visualization board is the most common tool associated with lean, and it can take a variety of forms. In a classic production environment, people often have cards for different production series that can be moved along a wire, starting when a market submits an order and finishing upon delivery.

5. **SEIRI:** sort, clean out, maintain order. Don't sweep anything under the rug – problems will slide back out to be solved. This is a sacred principle of lean. Japan has what is called the 5S program to eliminate different kinds of waste that lead to mistakes, and maybe even injuries. It is a way to achieve and maintain order and tidiness. In addition to *Seiri*, 5S consists of *Seiton* (structure), *Seiso* (shine, clean), *Seiketsu* (standardize) and *Shitsuke* (sustain). The essence here is to realize that actively forming good habits can be just as easy as falling into bad ones.

6. **HANSEI:** translates roughly to reflection, and is an essential concept in lean and the Toyota Way. Many people consider Toyota to be one of the best learning organizations around, and one key to their success is reflecting on mistakes and seeing them as learning opportunities. Making mistakes is only human, but they're often caused by system errors or deficient procedures. Every mistake is therefore considered a chance to improve conditions in order to do things the right way.

7. **MURI:** means not overloading an organization or an individual. A balanced workload and using everyone's creativity are key to lean culture; in fact, this is just as important as *Muda*. In addition, there is a third "M", *Mura*, which means having steady streams, rather than irregular streams with numerous hold-ups. Some organizations knowingly or unknowingly misunderstand and manipulate lean, and they quash *Muri* and *Mura*, streamlining to the extreme and overloading employees. While they may end up with even streams, that level of effort isn't sustainable in the long term. I would say that these organizations don't understand (or don't want to understand) what lean is really about.

4

WHAT IS LEAN AT HOME?

– a toolbox and philosophy for value-filled living

As I said before, lean at home evolved from pure survival instinct. Like many innovations, you could say it was simply chance. But chance is so often about taking advantage of coincidences – and our family needed tools to take control of our lives.

Lean at home is a way to obtain a smoothly flowing life, instead of wishing to escape. At our house, we achieved incredible results in just over a year. But if you want to see real, permanent change, work with lean at home long term.

First and foremost, lean at home means working with your most essential daily streams. Begin by thinking of all the streams in your home: see the entire thread, from an identified need to everything that happens before it is met. To be sure, it will become clear that a home is like an enormous needs factory: hungry bellies that need to be filled; dirty socks that need to be washed; parents of young children desperate for a full night's sleep; children who need structure, stability, security; students who need help with homework; bills that need to be paid; windows that need to be washed; school papers that need to be filled in; every possible and impossible decision, from electric companies to insurance policies; streamlined workplaces that require evening, night and weekend shifts at home; the need to steadily improve self-esteem; and last but not least, the need of each individual for self-actualization: to evolve as a person and have the chance to blossom.

I could write an entire book about needs, but this is a book about solutions. (I could also write an entire book on various escape strategies – endless daydreaming, too much overtime, indulging in a bit more wine than necessary, being more present in your next vacation than in this moment. But I'll leave that here, and continue to the solutions.)

A giant factory of needs

Can you see your home as a giant factory of needs? And can you see the benefits you would enjoy if you met true needs simply, efficiently, and with presence? Benefits like more time and money, a healthier environment, and harmonious daily living. By prioritizing your most important streams and organizing your home around them, such benefits can be realized. All homes may have unique challenges, but they also all have a flood of needs, and a real or perceived lack of time, money, energy, and resources, not to mention the finite resources of our environment.

It is often that very lack, real or perceived, that makes us come to a standstill. Makes us feel insufficient. Makes us feel guilty. Makes us ill, and causes divorces. But: it could be the opposite. Lean helps you liberate resources and eliminate bottlenecks. You'll have smooth processes, and you'll create conditions to achieve a sense of flow.

Kaizen (continuous improvements) will help you take control of your most important streams, which will catalyse change. It will help you find your own solutions to your own challenges. You'll find no long, worthless checklists that do nothing to help you meet your actual needs or live your dream life here. In lean, problems aren't only seen as negative; they're also considered opportunities in disguise. If you see your day-to-day life this way, you will eventually be less judgmental, more accepting, less stressed, and more inspired to actually get things done.

A lean home wastes nothing, and constantly striving to reduce waste is fundamental to lean. We're hard on the environment, and we waste our money. Lean reduces every aspect of waste. With lean at home, you will systematically review your wastefulness. You will establish goals, you will begin, and you will change – sustainably.

Close relationships

Let's return to our metaphor of the home as a needs factory: what materials are required? Everything from food, clothing and electricity, to love, dreams, and desires. Are we achieving those dreams, and nurturing the love we invest? It's palpable when you enter a home to which everyone contributes, a home that supports dreams and satisfies the needs of each family member. Our closest relationships help us evolve as people, but they can also cause us to come to a standstill, to get stuck in established roles, or to give up what we really want from life. Lean at home can help us achieve our goals, realize our dreams, and keep us from wasting the things we value most.

Visual management and planning are another fundamental pillar of lean. If there is one thing that every home needs, it is a common plan that is clear to everyone. It is impossible to assemble the puzzle of your lives if you can't see all the pieces, or if they are thrown at you from every direction, leaving you with the sense that you are under attack and out of control. Lean includes a concept called *Kanban*, which means "sign" in Japanese. In our home, we've made a *Kanban* board that signals to us what is coming up. The board presents all of us with the same information, and it includes everything that runs through our streams: budgets, bills to be paid, our goals and values, information for the home, incoming documents to be signed, school schedules and lunch menus, annual planning, and current events. But most importantly, it has a detailed, in-depth schedule of the next two weeks, to which anyone can add or make changes. Every Sunday evening, we review what's happening in the coming week and the week after that. This gives the kids a sense of predictability and expectation, and the grown-ups a sense of being in control.

Lean at home is also about reflecting on what a "good home" and "good daily living" mean to you. When Toyota Motor Company was founded in 1937, the management saw the company as a fragile, newly planted tree, and they asked themselves: what do we consider a beautiful tree? Then, each day, they reflected on the decisions they had made to help the tree grow stronger and more beautiful. So ask yourself: what do you consider a good home? What have you done today to make your home a little stronger, a little more beautiful? *Hansei* – reflection – includes looking back in order to learn and follow up what you've done (reflecting on whether you've met the most essential, basic needs of each family member), as well as looking forward. If you think in terms of an overall stream, what resources are necessary in a home, and what are you creating? Because whether you're conscious of it or not, you are creating something. Do you have in-depth discussions about what you want to achieve with your home, or are you so absorbed in renovating the kitchen or choosing colors for the new sofa that you've forgotten the things that matter most?

Lean at home in the phases of life

Lean at home works at every stage of life. It works if you live alone, but offers the most leverage for several people who live together and share (or should be sharing) responsibilities. When I write "you," sometimes I mean you as an individual, and sometimes I mean you as in the two of you, because your actual family situation is irrelevant. Lean at home works in different phases and different families, so adapt it based on your needs and conditions.

If you and your partner are moving in and starting a home together, you will build an incredible foundation by thinking about lean living, right from the start, and talking about what you believe a good home to be. If you have children, lean at home will help you create a harmonious home and be truly present while your kids are young. You will learn how to focus on streams and conscientiously fulfill the needs of each family member. Once the kids are older and can be more involved in housework, distribute responsibility for the home. Everyone should help reduce waste, and everyone should work on continuous improvements. Keep reviewing your goals, so that your home evolves at the same rate that life changes, and you can all achieve your dreams.

With lean at home, you will always be one step ahead. You will be prepared for evolving needs and conditions. And you will have a dynamic home, where everyone has the chance to contribute, be recognized, and bloom.

If you are in the process of divorce, lean at home can facilitate your work together in terms of the children, and can help establish a sense of security and predictability if they alternate homes. It will help you plan together and focus on your children's needs. With the help of visual tools like *Kanban*, you can keep track of all those practical details, from basketball shoes and other items that need to be transported between the two homes, to making sure your joint efforts work for everyone.

Lean at home can strengthen cooperation among children, grandchildren, and both sets of grandparents, so that they can help out to whatever extent they want and are able. Clear goals and good planning make it possible for everyone to work together towards the same end. Many cultures hold that parental responsibility isn't over until your grandchildren are grown, and you've passed on your ethics, wisdom, curiosity, sense of responsibility, and joie de vivre. Today, grandparents tend to be reduced to babysitter status, and we often lose that final all-important dimension of parenting.

The tree you planted will grow more branches, stronger branches – as long as its roots are securely anchored in good, nourishing soil.

Different conditions

Lean at home is about how to organize your home in order to better meet needs. By using the same methods to review streams that other organizations use, we can increase stream efficiency and free up energy in the home. But lean at home is not a method offering a single solution for everyone. It's a nearly 100-year-old concept in which you find lasting solutions to the problems of your unique lives yourselves; it's a way to acquire the tools necessary to start making changes.

Because what does an economically privileged family in a huge house have in common with a recently arrived immigrant family in a housing project? What does a forty-something couple with four teenagers in Nice have in common with a gay couple in New York City? What do they have in common with you and me? A lot more than may appear to be the case on the surface; to be sure, we have a tendency to focus on differences rather than on what unifies us. We may not have the same dreams – but we all have dreams. We have varying privileges in terms of resources – but we have all probably experienced an actual lack of time, money, and energy. We may all have different views of climate change and pollution, but we and future generations are equally dependent on our environment. We have needs – fundamental and developmental needs; we have problems, we have things we want to change. I have seen how lean at home can help people make the changes they need to create flow in their daily lives. Granted, lean at home offers the most to homes with several people under one roof, because the practice has so much to do with participation and consensus. But I have had feedback from many readers who live alone who have been inspired to work with lean at home, particularly with streams, *Kaizen* and methods for reducing waste.

Not like the emperor's new clothes

To avoid misinterpretations, I think it's important to describe what lean at home is not. It is **not** a fast, efficient method to create a home resembling a production process, where family members are internal customers. It is **not** a path to a dreary, practical, stripped-down, unimaginative, goal-oriented home where you do **not** live in the present moment. It is **not** a way to see your house or apartment only as something to be refined, endlessly tinkered with, repainted, renovated, and improved.

Nor is lean at home about immediately satisfying every need, or perceived need, that you, your partner, or your children may have. The home is everyone's responsibility; even two-year-olds can participate on their terms. Determine what your actual needs are and prioritize them. Focus on the ones that are significant.

Lean at home is not like the emperor's new clothes. Some business leaders reject lean at first, on the grounds that everything the philosophy involves should naturally be practiced already. But once they actually start working with it, patiently and intentionally, they see the potential and the point.

Nor is lean at home a pure streamlining philosophy to optimize your productivity or performance. Some workplaces are invaded by quacks who, whether consciously or unconsciously, grossly misunderstand and manipulate lean. They take streamlining to the extreme, they don't involve the true experts, and then they move on and disrupt the next workplace.

If you just use the tools, you will lose the soul of lean. If you just use the philosophy and skip the tools, you won't achieve results. But remember: you don't have to do it all at once. You don't even have to do it all in one lifetime. For now, the most important step is to work with a visual to clarify everything that is going on in your lives. It will help you reel in your most vital streams and change them (with the help of *Kaizen*) in order to transform waste into value and move from frustration to flow.

5

STREAMS

– how to move from frustration to flow

Does energy flow in your home and your life? Does your daily life run smoothly? Working with streams wisely will take you away from bottlenecks and a desire to escape. A sense of flow comes as an affirmation and a reward; as soon as you achieve it, you will want to experience it over and over again.

STREAM: that which takes place from the time a need arises until it is met. Metaphorically, think of a stream as a thread, with a beginning and an end.

FLOW: when time and space nearly cease to exist, and you lose yourself in what you are doing.

STREAM EFFICIENCY: measuring the value-creating time within your total stream time yields your stream efficiency. In other words, stream efficiency = value-creating time/turnaround time.

In actuality, achieving flow is fairly easy; you simply have to create the conditions for it.

Now, please read each line carefully.

Return to Sakichi Toyoda's thread metaphor, and remember: that which is moved forward and refined in a stream is a stream unit. Follow the entire journey: a bell pepper's trip from the market to being consumed in a fragrant goulash; a letter's trip from the mailbox to the recipient; a messy, sleepy two-year-old's journey towards bedtime. Imagine that each of these things has a tiny memory chip recording its entire journey. What would that recording look like? Where would you benefit the most from a change? Streams contain something value-creating, i.e. something in the stream unit is processed and meets a need. But much of what takes place in a stream does not meet a need, which means it can be pure waste.

In the case of the bill, the value-creating activity is the transaction: the actual paying of the bill. All the time spent searching for the envelope, sighing over the bill, and losing it again are simply extra work. That bell pepper may not become a goulash at all – how often does it end up rotting and being tossed in the garbage? (Statistically, every third time in western Europe.) Is the two-year-old's trip to bed full of tears, resistance, and crankiness, or is it intimate and trusting?

What creates value?

Waste generates frustration; therefore, we create value by eliminating waste from streams. Given that thinking in terms of streams is fundamental to lean, understanding how much of a stream's total time is actually value-creating is essential. To figure it out, let's turn for a moment to mathematics. Again, think of the thread: at one end, you have a need, and at the other, the need is met.

Turnaround time is how long a stream takes from start to finish, i.e. everything that happens from the moment a need is identified to the moment it is met. But we still don't know how efficient the stream is. To find out, simply calculate the stream efficiency. Expressed mathematically, it looks like this: stream efficiency = value-creating time/ turnaround time. Play with the idea that on average, it takes two weeks for a blouse to go from dirty to washed, ironed and hanging in the wardrobe (if it even is ironed or hung up). The actual turnaround time is two weeks = 14 days = 336 hours. The value-creating activity is the process of loading the clothes into the washing machine, starting the machine, emptying it, drying the laundry, ironing what needs ironing and hanging your clothing back up in the wardrobe. Let's call that about four hours. So, stream efficiency here is 4/336 = 1%.

Or think about your food stream: you get home from work and try to improvise a dinner you haven't planned out. First, you go impulse shopping with small, hungry children in tow after picking them up from school and daycare. You imagine the stress in the kitchen, and maybe you try to buy time with some toast, a piece of fruit, a few carrot sticks, or another snack for the kids, who eat lunch early at school and are starving by now. And then, full from their snack, they sit down at the dinner table and hardly touch the food you prepared through sweat and tears. Planning the meal, having the ingredients ready, and involving the kids in preparation would make the entire stream twice as value-creating.

The point here is that value-creation is what is valuable and important to you: anything from yoga, reading, playing, and eating chocolate to baseball, watching the news, and spending time with your kids. It's not about production, performance, or creating economic value. The point is to meet essential, basic needs for life, as well as to give and have space for self-actualization. Though it may seem like the opposite at first glance, in order to maintain a balanced life, it is value-creating to set limits with an employer who demands more and more work from you in your free time. If you have a seat in the sun with a cup of coffee in the morning, you should enjoy it. If you spend that moment dwelling and feeling guilty because you're not being productive, then it's a waste of time, but if you decide to relax in the sunshine, listen to the birds, and be present with your choice, it will be value-creating. If you feel as though you've had a moment of intimacy with your baby, rather than struggling to get her to fall asleep according to the five-minute method, then that is value-creating. Think about what creates value, and stand up for it – with yourself and others.

Heavy and tiresome

What is the current state of your streams at home? To begin, analyse your home and identify where you spend your time, energy, and money, and where things slow down and become heavy and tiresome. Where do anxiety and destructive stress arise? What weighs on your wallet and the environment? Start with the stream that is most in need of a change.

Then try out a simplified version of *Kaizen*: review your current situation, think about how you wish the stream was, and determine what you need to do to get there. It may sound more complicated than it really is. Remember the metaphor of a thread running through an organization. Where does the thread begin, where does it end, what happens in between, where is value created, and where does stress form? Here, it makes sense to go over what sucks up the most energy, and where you have the most to gain by making a change.

For example, think about your clothing thread. How do you take care of your clothes? Do you have them "just in time," when you need them? How does the stream look? The clothing thread begins when you shop for, or inherit, clothes that (in the best case) meet a need. Naturally, the goal is for the clothes to be the right size, undamaged, and clean when someone needs them, whether it's a waterproof jacket for the rain, a gown for the party, or a favorite fleece. The thread ends when the clothes are outgrown and either given away, or completely threadbare and ready to be thrown away.

Follow the clothing stream and everything that happens in the process, from beginning to end. How does your clothing account look? What happens in your wash stream? How many piles of laundry form before everything is cleaned, ironed, and put away? How many times does someone ask for certain clothes before you find them dirty, wrinkled, or even outgrown? Once old clothes are sorted out, do you donate or sell them? How many spaces around your home have various kinds of clothing storage?

Remember, the fashion industry is the second-most polluting industry after oil. We live in a world of fast fashion, where companies produce high volumes of low-priced clothing at the expense of the environment.

From chaos to creativity

Think about your exercise stream: do you have bottlenecks before you get started, or like a fireman, can you just throw on your gear and get out for a run? How often do you lose inspiration because you can't find your exercise clothes, your bike has a flat tyre, or your swimsuit is in the wash? Or your kids' homework stream: is there an inspiring place with sharp pencils, an eraser, and a good lamp where the kids can sit in peace and quiet and concentrate? Where they can have a nice balance of solitude and available help if needed?

And your food stream: how can you make your chaotic grocery store trips with the kids more creative, and value-creating? How can you get rid of wastefulness? It doesn't require that much planning.

This is what lean is all about: reviewing your streams and thinking through how you want them to be, then creating the conditions to make it so. Anxiety is rarely caused by the actual value-creating **activity**; rather, it's our **approach** to the entire process, with all the piles, bottlenecks, and mistakes that cause unrest.

An organization can be described as a main process or thousands of subprocesses. In lean at home, it's important to consider your main features and keep them simple. For example, the smartest approach is to think of the overall clothing stream, rather than dividing it up into a ton of substreams.

But how you choose to design the interface is up to you. When I lecture about this, I often describe it as zooming in and out of a stream. If your primary stress factor is nightly dinners, focus on that stream. If your morning routines are chaotic, focus on them: from the challenging art of leaving a cosy bed to the time you reach your school or workplace. Or perhaps your organization and tidiness stream: what should be your rules for taking things out in common spaces? Have piles of unread books and magazines invaded your home?

Identify your bottlenecks and create conditions for change.

How to do laundry ten times more efficiently

To demonstrate just how inefficient our laundry stream was, let me paint a picture for you. Imagine a child's shirt on its way to being washed, ironed, and hung up in the wardrobe. Before implementing lean in our home, this is how long this dreaded stream took. You might assume that two adults, one a doctor and the other a VP, would be able to stay on top of a simple task like the laundry, but when we analyzed our stream, we were ashamed.

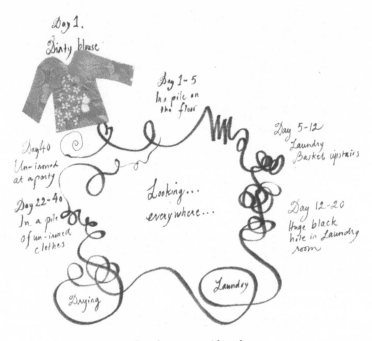

Day 1.
Dirty blouse

Day 1-5
In a pile on
the floor

Day 5-12
Laundry
Basket upstairs

Day 40
Un-ironed
at a party

Day 22-40
In a pile
of un-ironed
clothes

Looking...
everywhere...

Day 12-20
Huge black
hole in Laundry
room

Drying

Laundry

Our laundry stream without lean
We had lots of clothes lost in piles. Once they were
finally washed, rarely were they ironed or hung up.

First, the shirt landed in a pretty little pile of dirty and clean clothes in
one of the kids' rooms, and there it stayed for around five days. Then,
after I nagged and shouted, it would move to the overflowing laundry
basket in the upstairs bathroom, where it would stay for about a week
before ending up in the laundry room in the basement two floors down,
tossed atop a heaping pile of colors, whites, delicates, and synthetics.

It could stay there anywhere from five days to three weeks.

We dreaded going down to the laundry room. Just the thought of beginning to sort through those wretched piles made us ache for an excuse
to escape. Starting the washing machine, which only took a couple of
minutes, wasn't the problem. The bottleneck of tasks created by doing
the laundry posed the true hurdle.

Once the shirt was finally washed, it wouldn't be hung up immediately. No, it would land in a chest with the other clothes waiting for us
to set up the ironing board with the lovely, seldom-used steam iron.

The shirt could be in the ironing chest for a long time. We ironed about once a month, at which time we managed to get through about a quarter of the clothes that lay hidden in the chest – the garments at the bottom of the stack hadn't been ironed in years. Sometimes, the kids grew out of clothes before we even washed and ironed them a single time.

Essentially, you could say that our turnaround time was about 40 days, which is 960 hours.

In other words, the amount of waste was enormous, and we royally failed to satisfy the need of finding the clothes we needed "just in time" – despite the fact that we had invested a fairly sizable sum on clothing. And having all of our lovely clothes in piles was certainly not the optimal way to take care of them.

Stream efficiency was very, very low. The actual value-creating activity – washing, drying, and ironing – took around four hours. Four hours divided by 960 hours ($4/960 = 0.004$) is a stream efficiency of 0.4%. That's about how long our average laundry time once was.

The cost of clutter

All of those piles of clothes took up tons of floor space, more than 10 square meters of floor space, in fact – and how much is that worth? Where we live in Stockholm, every square meter is worth around $5,400 which means ten wasted square meters is worth $54,000. Suddenly, our piles had a price tag. Living space is one of the most expensive things we invest in, whether we're paying rent or a mortgage.

Last but not least, we were so frustrated, annoyed, and even ashamed of our inability to take care of our clothing. Frustration was just the beginning. That's often the case when you start looking at streams: you realize that it isn't the activity itself that poses a challenge, but your approach to it. There are barriers and lead times. We had so much extra work in the form of sorting, re-sorting, moving piles, sometimes rewashing clothing. For kicks, we started timing some of those activities, and we learned that they didn't take particularly long – so why did we find them so grueling?

After taking control of the stream with *Kaizen*, it now takes four days max for a shirt to go from dirty to ironed and hanging in the wardrobe. Simple math shows that our laundry stream is ten times faster than before, and we usually have clothes when we need them. In our home, we've had countless examples of this kind of stream improvement. Once you get going, the process continues automatically.

I sincerely hope your laundry stream is leaner than ours was, but consider how many piles you have – what makes it so challenging to get that stream under control? Laundry seems like a minor detail in life, but according to Newstrategist research, we spend nearly three years of our lives washing clothes – so it's worthwhile investing some time and thought into making it more fun!

Break down barriers

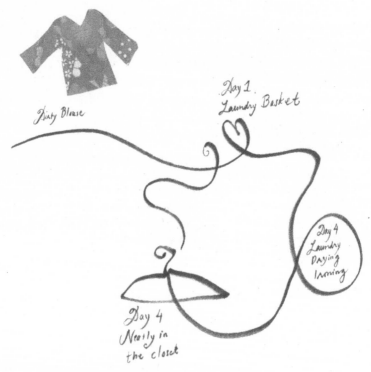

Dirty Blouse

Day 1
Laundry Basket

Day 4
Laundry
Drying
Ironing

Day 4
Neatly in
the closet

Our laundry stream with lean
With no piles of clothes everywhere, we have freed up our living space.

In the stream I describe above, a material was moved through the stream: clothing. The beginning of the thread is the need that arose to buy, wear, wash, iron, hang in the wardrobe, mend, and use a particular garment, and the end was the garment becoming worn out or too small, and subsequently sold/donated/thrown away. In a car company's case, it is always materials that are transported and then transformed into cars. In the example with the two women who discovered lumps in their breasts (*see* page 12), the tissue samples are transported in order to get a diagnosis. At home, the material stream may be food to be purchased, stored, and transformed into delicious, nutritious and fun meals.

It could also be a recycling stream. How do we make sure we recycle everything that can be recycled, and how do we get the kids to participate as a matter of course? The recycling stream is fairly easy to get under control, and it reduces our environmental footprint; plus, we no longer have garbage floating around our home, only to finally end up in the ordinary trash anyway. Through lean living you move towards having a circular home (circular economy is a system aimed at minimizing waste and making the most of resources).

What about your exercise stream? Do you value exercise, but never hit the gym? Before, the fact that I could rarely find my gym shoes or swimsuit blocked me. Now that we've reviewed our exercise stream, our whole family's gym shoes and exercise gear are hung up and aired out in the basement, so it's easy for us to get out and go. It used to take at least fifteen minutes to find everything, and by then, the desire to work out had often dissipated.

Eliminate the barriers. When you go over a stream, you're likely to find lengthy throughput times and long, narrow bottlenecks to navigate before you can begin the value-creating task. Such barriers fuel anxiety and negative feelings, and demand a lot of energy – that's about as far from flow as you can get. It's the definition of anti-flow.

From smoothness to flow

So far, we've talked about working past the frustration stage and getting things done smoothly. Next comes the art of laying the groundwork to occasionally achieve flow, that euphoric sense of concentration, of time ceasing to exist. Achieving flow is rewarding; it's almost intoxicating. If you've ever felt it, you'll want to feel it again. You'll be able to joyfully embark upon chores over and over...

But is it really possible to achieve a sense of flow in everything we do? Combined with an intentional effort to be in the present moment, lean at home makes it much likelier to happen. Flow doesn't only occur during sports or creative processes. It can happen when you make pancakes, hang pictures, prune roses, do homework with the kids, or anything else you can think of.

You can't fight your way to flow, but you can create the conditions to get there, and that's exactly what lean is about: creating conditions for smooth processes, and occasionally achieving a sense of flow.

Different analyses and studies have tried to show how athletes achieve flow. A clear correlation exists between high self-confidence and minimal negative thoughts, low levels of anxiety, a positive inner monologue, and a solid understanding of your abilities. People who achieve flow tend to be internally motivated and driven by their own goals.

How often is that the case for you at home? Do you have a high level of self-confidence and positivity, and not many negative thoughts about chores?

A feeling of flying

The illustration on the following page shows a classic model for flow, as designed by Hungarian psychologist Mihály Csíkszentmihályi. It consists of two axes, skill and challenge, which form four fields. If skill and challenge are both low, apathy results rather than flow. If challenge is high and skill is low, fear results; if challenge is low and skill is high, boredom results. Flow may occur in the upper right quadrant, when a challenging task is met with a high skill level.

You can achieve fundamental smoothness in the flow quadrant if you create sensible conditions and calibrate your expectations.

Where are you when it comes to meeting the needs of the home? Focus on the most important streams. Where would you gain the most from a change?

I used to feel apathetic regularly, and it took time for me to begin various chores at home. Once I finally started, the task was laced with boredom and tinged with thoughts like *I'm not very good at this*.

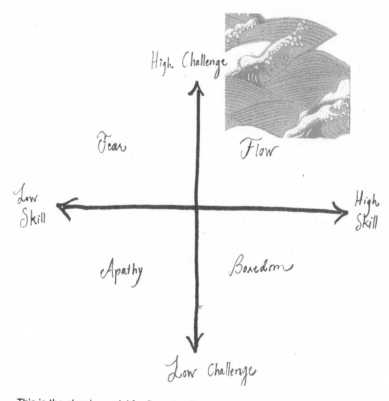

High Challenge

Fear

Flow

Low Skill

High Skill

Apathy

Boredom

Low Challenge

This is the classic model for flow: the flow quadrant. When you are in the upper right corner there is flow potential, so why not try to move to that quadrant, both at work and at home? Once you've experienced flow, you will want to experience it again and again; you are neither bored, nor stressed, nor worried. Remember, you cannot fight your way to flow, but you can create the conditions. Research shows that a clear correlation exists between high self-confidence and minimal negative thoughts, low levels of anxiety, a positive inner monologue, and a solid understanding of one's abilities.

Making pancakes has always been an ordeal for me. In my mind, I see the thin, gorgeous pancakes my mom made so well, but then I stand at the stove with a lumpy batter that sticks to the pan. After seeking advice from my mom (which took three minutes), I experienced flow at last: with help from the kids, two frying pans, and the ideal sized ladle for pancake perfection, all systems were go. I had the skill, I had a fairly challenging task, and those pancakes were the loveliest I had seen in pancake history.

Achieving flow affirms that you have set appropriate demands. Flow is unlikely to occur if your expectations are too high or too low. Csíkszentmihályi, who coined the term "flow" and studied it his entire life, defines flow as ego falling away and time flying. You are present, and use your knowledge to the fullest extent.

Baby steps

It is sad to see how many of us destroy our children's ability to intuitively experience flow. They may well be completely engrossed in what they're doing, and neither hear nor see what is happening around them. But often, we become frustrated with our children when they are in this state, which we interpret as a sign of indifference; we raise them to be on their toes and responsive. I now try to see it as a gift when my kids are totally absorbed in what they're doing, even if it doesn't fit my agenda at that moment. That sense of flow should be maintained as long as possible, and we grown-ups can learn something from the kids in this arena; we can be consumed by a task with them. Taking baby steps to nursery, climbing a tree, or wrapping a wreath of autumn leaves is easier if you feel that you're in control, rather than constantly under pressure.

Norwegian journalist Åsne Seierstad has said many wise things, but one quote in particular has stayed with me: "Think about what you enjoyed doing as a child. That is the key to your adult life." Try to let go of all the expected answers, your compulsion to be good, and every standard response about what makes you feel best.

> **Moving from frustrating to smooth processes, and occasionally achieving flow, step-by-step**
>
> Does energy flow through your home, or do you feel drained? Do your efforts to meet all the needs in your home run smoothly? Do you experience a sense of flow once in a while?
>
> 1. Reflect for a little while. Where do things slow down? What causes frustration and irritation? The laundry stream? The budget? The information stream, which may be overflowing? Meal planning? Cleaning? Recycling, or organization? Perhaps some other stream entirely? Think of streams as threads, each with a beginning and an end, and consider what happens along the way. Where are the tight bottlenecks, where are the barriers?

2. Consider the reverse, too – where do things run smoothly, and why? How can you apply what you do in those streams to other situations?

3. Look at the flow quadrant and home in on your most important streams, the processes that need to change. Think about what is required to move to flow.

4. Choose the stream that would benefit the most from a change. Start there. It's important to not do everything at once. Begin with one stream and finish it before you start the next one.

5. Once you've chosen a stream, analyse the present: how are things today? Think about why the situation is the way it is. If your analysis is careless, you risk only seeing the symptoms rather than the fundamental problem. If you don't get to the root of the problem, you will never solve it long-term.

6. Where in the stream is the actual improvement, i.e. what specifically is the value-creating activity? Once you find it, time it. For example, in the laundry stream, how long does it take to do the actual washing, drying and ironing? Or the bedtime stream – how long does it truly take for those tiny, tangled, messy, sleepy kids to brush their hair, brush their teeth, wash, and put on their pajamas?

7. Compare the value-creating activity to the entire turnaround time: divide the value-creating time by the amount of time the entire stream takes. From the time that blouse is dirty to the time it's hanging back up in the wardrobe, what requires energy? Is it all the piles and lead times, or that feeling of having too much to do? Or is it the actual value-creating activity that sucks up energy? Rather than the process itself, it's often the approach and bottlenecks that are draining.

8. Next, sketch out how you want things to be and what you need to get there. What new habits and procedures should you start with? Give *Kaizen* a try; see Chapter 6.

9. Lean is very much about trial and error. Analysis is important, but so is beginning quickly once you've reviewed the present situation and why it is as it is. Go from analysis to action within a few days (short lead times!). Otherwise, a barrier will pop up: the feeling that you ought to start over.

10. By creating the right conditions and expectations, you can go from smooth processes to a sense of flow – where time and space nearly disappear. When things are running smoothly, there is momentum and steady progress. But when they culminate in a sense of concentration, euphoria, timelessness – that is flow. The key is to meet a high challenge with a high skill level.

6

KAIZEN

– from problem to opportunity

A legendary lean leader once said, "Not having any problems is the biggest problem of all." Rather than seeing problems as negative, he saw them as opportunities in disguise. I think there's something beautiful about that.

FIVE IMPORTANT STEPS

Kaizen means continuous improvements, and simply put, it consists of five steps.

STEP ONE: describe the current situation, how things are today and why.

STEP TWO: agree on the desired future situation, how you want things to be.

STEP THREE: decide upon a new routine, one that is easy to do correctly.

STEP FOUR: start practicing the new routine within the same week. Write down the other suggestions for improvement so you can implement them as you move forward.

STEP FIVE: follow up. Make sure all of your changes are lasting and sustainable.

Kaizen is a concept in lean that refers to continuous, sustainable change. It's about not letting a day pass without making some kind of improvement – taking one of those many small steps. *Kaizen* is a contrast to stagnation; it is diametrically opposite to the strategy of waiting for a crisis to strike, then questioning and rejecting everything. Anyone who has worked with crisis management knows the enormous energy it requires, and how long it takes to recover. A crisis often has a high cost. But choosing to see problems as opportunities in disguise instead of annoyances will allow you to take a fresh approach, an approach that will serve as a catalyst to get things done. It is magical.

Current situation

Start by considering how things are today, and take pictures or a video for reference. Describe the current situation. Once processes begin to run smoothly, it can be easy to forget how they used to be. The same way we can become accustomed to messiness, order and tidiness become inherent after a while. Time how long various tasks take, and calculate your environmental footprint. Then you can celebrate your results.

When we went through the clothing stream (or, as I sometimes call it, our fashion flow) in our home, we mapped it out in a table. I'm presenting it here to show how simple it is (you don't need a fancy Excel spreadsheet).

Mattias and I sat down to describe the current situation and figure out our desired future situation. In lean, analysing *how* and *why* things are the way they are is essential to truly understanding the source of the problem, not just the symptoms. It's also important to be able to set up fairly measurable goals. So during our week or so of Clothing *Kaizen*, we set aside time to describe the situation. The kids were involved, too. Shown here in a table, late spring of 2011 was like this:

ANALYSIS OF THE CURRENT SITUATION	TIME/MONEY/AREA
Monthly spending on shoes and clothes for the entire family	About $700/month
Percentage of clothes in our home we use	20% of all clothing
Percentage of shoes in our home we use	30% of all shoes
Number of clothing piles in our home (laundry, ironing, damaged, unsorted, washed) Total square meter area	18–20 gloriously messy piles of clothes In total, various clothing piles occupying 10–15 square meters of our house
Average time it takes to get clothes washed, dried, ironed, and hanging in the wardrobe	About 40 days
Time it takes to hang clothes in the drying cabinet without a dryer (kids' socks, underwear, etc.)	An average of 10–15 minutes, depending on what the laundry load contains
First impression of the home – our hallway	The hall is cluttered with clothes and shoes, often a challenge to navigate
Use of hand-me-downs	Way too low

Our dream situation

While counting piles of clothing, calculating our average laundry time, estimating our clothing costs, and so on, we sketched our desired future situation, which is step two. How did we want our clothing stream to be?

The dream was to have our clothes "just in time," whether it was a pair of jeans, a pretty ruffled dress or a favorite fleece. We wanted to be rid of all twenty piles of clothes, and manage the laundry smoothly. We also wanted to be better at using hand-me-downs, caring for our clothes, mending them when they were damaged, and ensuring someone could inherit them when they got too small. Finally, we wanted to cut our spending on clothes and shoes by more than half.

Scenario: A family's morning stream without lean*

The word "Hurry!" echoes throughout the apartment where a couple lives with their two children (seven and eight years old). The morning stream that sets everyone up for the rest of the day was broken and inconsistent, just a tired transportation from bed to desk. This is the perspective of the mother, the project leader of the family. The flow starts from the time she finally falls asleep at 1am after scrolling through everyone's picture-perfect lives on Instagram. Five hours later, the alarm wakes her up and she starts immediately checking her work emails before a leisurely ten-minute shower to wake herself up.

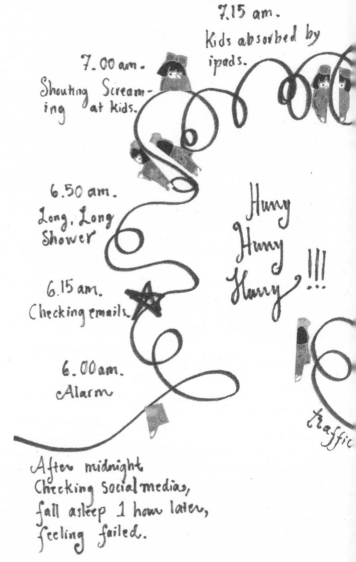

7.15 am.
Kids absorbed by ipads.

7.00 am.
Shouting Scream-ing at kids.

6.50 am.
Long, Long Shower

Hurry Hurry Hurry ?!!!...

6.15 am.
Checking emails.

6.00am.
Alarm

Traffic

After midnight Checking social medias, fall asleep 1 hour later, feeling failed.

---

* The scenarios included in this book are based on the real-life experiences of readers who have shared their journeys through lean with me.

Partner take
car to work.

Breakfast alone...

Breakfast left
at table....

7.25 am
Searching everything
everywhere...

7.50 am
Car nr 2 to school

stuck in traffic queue
#

9.15 am.
Arriving at
work. Frustrated.

Her mind elsewhere the whole time, she shouts at her kids to hurry. In her haste, she
forgets their homework and drops them off late to school. When she finally arrives at
work, she is distracted by thoughts of her children, their lateness and forgotten homework. When she arrives home in the evening, she is welcomed by that morning's mess:
breakfast dishes on the table and unmade beds, which makes her angry at her partner,
who avoided having any responsibility. It was a vicious circle that needed to end.

am
for
forgot
homework

How we got there

In step three, you develop ideas to get you from where you are now to your desired situation. It involves taking the time to create the right routines and habits. If the procedures are in place, if they're easy to do correctly, and if everyone tries, then you have the conditions for a lean home.

The point is to come up with suggestions together: parents assume joint leadership to see the changes through, and children participate. This was worth gold for us, because like most people who live together, we had slightly different approaches to tackling tasks. I usually spent months talking about what could be done, fairly obsessively, in all honesty. But I carefully thought through my ideas before ever implementing them. Mattias was the opposite: he considered briefly, and then he made a change. I might suddenly come home to a brand new shelf somewhere, or a clever fabric rolling storage system.

It was truly a waste of time: because I hadn't been involved at all, I often thought these were stupid, expensive ideas. In fact, we complement one another, but our lack of communication made us counterproductive – like many others.

When instead, we sat down together to consider different solutions, we had much more fun and our ideas were better.

Now we have a shared list that we both check off, which offers the benefit of letting us switch tasks. Now I can find the toolbox (I used a drill for the first time in my 42 years, and achieved blissful flow) and Mattias may soon learn how to turn on the sewing machine. We've gradually started rewriting our gender contract at home, which we hope will leave an impression on our son and two daughters.

When one of us goes down to hammer something in the basement, it's no longer with irritation and anxiety: we know what's going on and look forward to the solution. Slowly, securely, and patiently, we're unmasking opportunities in disguise. The following table shows our ideas for improving our fashion flow.

SUGGESTIONS FOR IMPROVEMENT	RESULTS
Establish a planned stream with a clear beginning and end: wash, dry, iron, and put away	Throughput time: 4–8 hours depending on the wash program
Compare the energy use of a drying cabinet and a dryer to decide whether we should invest in a new appliance	Investment: $1,200 for an energy efficient tumble dryer
Purge the laundry room, so that it only contains clean clothes and an ironing board	✓
Dressing room – fix up as a kid's room for Samuel	✓
Shop secondhand	✓
Clearly labeled boxes of hand-me-downs, each containing a single size	✓
Shoe storage box in the hallway	✓
Clearly labeled seasonal storage	✓
Sewing machine and kit	✓
Basement entrance with work clothes, boots, etc. close to the drying cabinet	✓

Get started

Essential to *Kaizen* is step four, when you actually begin to implement some changes during *Kaizen* Week. This is the time to make your vision a reality. Don't stop at notes on paper – get the ball rolling, and keep going. Otherwise, a new bottleneck may arise: starting over, which can almost be like starting over from the very beginning. So make sure to begin with a few changes the first week, and make a "to finish" list that prioritizes what and how you will continue with the rest. Work together to prioritize and check items off your list.

Freed-up space	Cleared 30 square meters total (including the piles of clothes and the dressing room). At Stockholm prices, that's the equivalent of $150,000 worth of living space.
Average time for a dirty garment to be washed, dried, ironed, and rep- laced in the wardrobe	From our previous average of 40 days to about 4 days. When a laundry bag is full, we wash it. It's a bottleneck-free stream.
Savings: time	Laundry is 10 times more efficient.
Savings: money	$460–$530 less in monthly costs for clo- thes and shoes.
Savings: the environ- ment	We'll decrease our environmental footprint a bit once we've saved for an energy- efficient tumble dryer, which will be kinder than our old, inefficient drying cabinet.
Clothes "just in time"	We now have most clothes when we need them. The kids have extra clothes at school and daycare, and the days of fin- ding a lone sock or glove are gone.

Follow up

Step five: follow up to make sure your changes are lasting and sus- tainable. This will prevent you from having a hailstorm of activities that melt away, rather than becoming permanent changes.

Kaizen is a lifestyle. Rather than taking urgent measures, you'll be able to focus your energy on simplifying, improving, and keeping everything running smoothly. We emptied the old ironing chest (we gave away some of the clothes at the bottom that we'd nei- ther missed nor touched in years), painted it a beautiful shade of bronze, and replaced it with four bags: one each for delicates, col- ors, white loads, and one for black clothes. The bags are perfectly sized for the washing machine. Everyone, even two-year-old Samuel, learned where to put their dirty laundry right away. When a bag is full enough, we take it down to the laundry room, which is now the laundry, ironing, and tailoring room. There are no dirty clothes here, just clean laundry. When we bring down a bag, we load its contents into the washing machine immediately, and we dry and iron the clothes in a simple stream with a clear beginning and end. A simple hole in a trouser knee gets a patch ironed on immediately, and the job is done right the first time – not quickly and sloppily, so that it just falls off with the first wear. Right away. Create the right procedures so you can perform value-adding activities, not tons of unnecessary work.

We bought an energy-efficient tumble dryer, which will save us about 15 minutes for each load (the time it takes to hang everything up in the big drying cabinet). That will eliminate another bottleneck. We do laundry at least six times a week, which means we'll save 1.5 hours per week by using a dryer instead of a drying cabinet. We will also reduce our energy consumption with a new, energy-efficient dryer.

Opportunities in disguise

It makes sense to start with what generates the most frustration and sucks up the most time. Simply put: start wherever you have the most to gain from a change. Spend time creating the right conditions and procedures. The important thing is to actually start implementing a few urgent changes before the week is out. After that, you'll have a list left over of more things you want to improve. This is your *Kaizen* list, and you'll use it to make a small change each day. You'll stop being reactive, and you will see how things can be refined. If you time these processes, you'll see that they don't take that long, and they are satisfying. Here are some of the small, satisfying changes we've made that only take fifteen minutes: we've arranged all of our cookbooks by color; we've put all wooden utensils in the kitchen in a pretty ceramic bowl; we have a beautiful sewing box; our hairbrushes are in a rubber band by the mirror, so we know right where they are; we've labeled all of our shoe storage boxes with names, so we don't use the wrong one; we have a special cupboard in the hall with a clothes brush and shoe polish (even for the kids); we have a line for hanging up exercise clothing in the basement, so we can easily throw on our gear and go. We've assembled an inviting, inspiring craft box with everything from beads, brushes, fabrics, old paper towel rolls, and more to use for crafting. We've replaced the clutter of multiple boxes of different teas and loose teabags with a single gorgeous box that we pick up reverently whenever it's time for a cup.

Scenario: A family's morning stream with lean

With the help of *Kaizen* the family agreed how they wanted to change the morning stream together. The children had just learned how to cycle. They looked at a map of the area and worked out how one of the parents could cycle with the children to school and then on to work instead of driving. They sold one of their cars, reducing their carbon footprint. The other parent now takes public transport, using this free time to listen to audiobooks. They have agreed as a family not to use their mobile phones or tablets in the morning apart from as an alarm. Together they have transformed waste to value, and the morning stream has become something they look forward to.

7.00 am
A wake-up hug

11.00 pm
Fall asleep

Harmon

t
gether

7.40 Braid, brush....

8.00 Bike to school
with kids

8.45 At the
office, ready to
work!

Lots of small steps make life simpler and more beautiful. Putting together a sewing box may sound trivial, but our sewing tools used to be sloppily tossed in a broken box, a mess of endlessly tangled spools of thread. I invested in a lovely, functional sewing box. I collected thread and finally dared to use my grandmother's mother-of-pearl thimble, with its incredibly delicate gold embellishments. Now I long to take out the sewing box to mend clothes, sew on buttons, and fix Barbie outfits. The hurdle of untangling threads and finding needles is gone, replaced with the simple desire for a sensual thimble, already in its place in the sewing box.

Use simple solutions that make life easier. They can be beautiful solutions, too, things that inspire you and make you happy. Ellen Key, a Swedish writer born in 1849, said that a home doesn't have a soul until whoever lives there lets her soul show. Lean at home isn't about gloom, functionality, or everything being stripped down. If you need beauty – and most people do – then find it.

But continuous improvements do not mean continuous work. You don't have to be Oscar the Grouch, constantly grumbling and stomping around like a janitor. Be present with what you're doing right now, but don't think you have to finish before you can start living your life. The work is never done.

Beginning continuous improvements, step-by-step – *Kaizen*

1. When, as described in Chapter 5, you have clearly identified which stream in your home would most benefit from a change, do a *Kaizen* exercise: describe the current situation (how things are and why), agree on a future situation, and develop new procedures. They should be easy to do right.

2. It's important to start your changes immediately during *Kaizen* Week. If you do, the ball will be rolling and you will have jumped the first hurdle.

3. Take "before" pictures so you can remember how your home looked before you began making improvements. It can be easy to forget how untidy and messy things were before you made changes.

4. Try to see problems as opportunities in disguise. Try to be inspired instead of irritated, and to be accepting instead of anxiously making comparisons.

5. Make a "to-finish" list of improvement ideas you didn't start in week one, and check them off as you complete them.

6. It's essential to define the beginning and end of the improvements you choose to make; don't start something else before you've completed earlier improvements. Having lots of unfinished projects under way is incredibly draining, while completing a single task will give you an energy boost. See one beginning and one end, and split big projects into realistic, achievable goals.

7. The most important step is to monitor to make sure all of your changes are lasting and sustainable.

8. Celebrate the improvements you make. Continuous improvement doesn't mean continuous work – it means continuous celebrations. Relax and enjoy your results; don't constantly think about what needs to be done. Be present in the moment.

7

MUDA

– from waste to value

Eliminating waste is directly linked to having good streams at home. Because everything in lean at home – and in your home – is connected. Good flows will help you reduce waste and better manage resources, like time, money, the environment, and love. And reducing waste is what this essential pillar, Muda, is all about. It's actually rather simple: by creating a more sustainable home, we can create a more sustainable community and nurture respect for our limited resources.

According to lean, value streams (all that happens from the time a need arises to the time it is satisfied) contain **eight types of waste**. Two of the most notable reasons for waste are overproduction and lack of participation. In lean at home, I've translated the former to overconsumption. The other types of waste are waiting, inventory, extra work, reworking, transportation, and unnecessary movement and steps.

How much time and money do you spend on unnecessary consumption? How much space do unnecessary things take up in your home? How much time do you require to take care of those things? How often do you buy something you don't really need, with money you don't have, to impress people you may not care about that much?

Sure, we consume to meet needs – real, basic needs that are necessary for survival (like food), needs that are necessary to function in school and society, and certain needs that we had no idea we had until the advertiser's message flashed in front of us. Indeed, how many of the needs we experience are so-called compensatory needs? That new top, the latest iPhone, a bigger house, a renovated kitchen? Needs that feel crucial, that we're willing to sacrifice so much to meet, but that maybe don't compensate for a basic need that isn't being fulfilled? In many cases, compensatory needs are merely a manifestation of pure wastefulness. And worst of all, we may sacrifice some of our more important basic needs to meet them (like sleep, exercise, security, clean air, time spent with loved ones – the list goes on and on).

Lean at home can also help you step up participation by putting everyone's ideas, creativity and willingness to lend a hand to good use. Lean encourages shared practical, emotional, and financial responsibility. Participation absolutely includes kids. You may need to remind yourself once in a while that kids want to pitch in and work together, but remember, it's up to you, the adult, to encourage them and nurture their sense of community with tasks they can complete on their own terms. Chapter 11 offers more in-depth information about how lean at home helps increase participation at home.

Eight kinds of waste

One way to begin is by identifying your wastefulness in terms of the eight types of waste as defined by lean.

1. **OVERPRODUCTION** – in lean, this means producing more, faster or earlier than necessary. In lean at home, I've translated this to **overconsumption:** we buy more and consume faster than we need to. Eastern philosophers often talk about the importance of traveling light. *How much do you consume that you don't really need, with money you don't really have?*

2. **LACK OF PARTICIPATION** and untapped creativity are often the biggest causes of waste at the workplace and at home. Too little participation from the kids or insufficient involvement from a partner take their toll. *How much participation is there in your home?*

3. **INVENTORY** – how much unnecessary stuff do you have at home? Clutter everywhere wastes time and energy – and makes you feel guilty for not taking care of it. *If you look around your house, how many of your belongings do you really need, and how many truly have sentimental value? How much living space does everything take up? Remember that living space is probably one of the most valuable things you own. Are you wasting it? How much energy do you waste heating unused living space that has become storage space? And how much does that cost every year?*

4. **WAITING** – how much time do we waste waiting for our family? I believe that it's important to be aware of children's ability to be present and mindful, which is something we can be better at, too. Have a schedule so that wait time can be value-creating. *Who do you have to wait for in your family, and why? Do other people have to wait for you?*

5. **EXTRA WORK** – having to do unnecessary things because the original need wasn't met, like paying late fees, or raking up a harvest from the entire garden after a windstorm, because you didn't pick the fruit from the trees. The worst thing is that we often feel like we're doing something value-creating when we do extra work. *How much extra work do you do at home?*

6. **REWORKING** – redoing things that were done wrong; correcting. Instead, spend some time laying the foundation to make it easy to do things right the first time. *How often do you have to redo something because you were sloppy the first time? How much information do you have to reread because you didn't take it in the first time? Do you redo each other's work – for example, if one of you loaded the dishwasher does the other reorganize the dishes before they are washed?*

7. **TRANSPORTATION** – unnecessary transportation to various activities, school, nursery, or to pick up a forgotten grocery item.

Do you coordinate the kids' activities? Do you help out your neighbors by taking their kids to school, too? Do you carpool? Do you ever walk to work instead of sitting in traffic jams?

8. **UNNECESSARY MOVEMENT AND STEPS** – such as looking for things. *How much time do you spend looking for things in a week? Make a list of the top ten things you most often have to look for, then decide where to keep them, once and for all.*

Consider how your wastefulness is manifested. Here are some examples of how things can be – sad statistics that show the average situation if you are a consumer living in a first-world country.

» You are likely to waste one-third of all the food you buy. Most of it is edible when thrown away.

» You use around one-fifth of all your clothing.

» Your environmental footprint is huge. If everyone in the world used the same amount of natural resources used by the average consumer in a first-world country, we would need four, or even five, planet Earths in order to accommodate the impact on the planet.

» You forsake important basic needs to meet compensatory needs, and allow idealistic marketing messages to control your spending habits.

The "5 Whys" – *Hadome*

It's pretty easy to see where you have waste, but it can be harder to understand why and determine the root cause. You can use the "5 Whys" method, which is called *Hadome* in lean.

The purpose of the "5 Whys" is to rule out those initial, perceived root causes that are actually symptoms. Truly solving the problem requires understanding and coming to a reasonable agreement on its root cause.

What is just as important as asking "why" several times? Stopping in time. If you ask "why" too many times, you'll get away from the problem.

A movie I once saw depicted the problem posed by asking "why" too many times. In the film, a little girl gets up at five a.m., wakes up her dad, and together, they sit in the kitchen and talk. Energetically munching on toast, she drives her father crazy as she asks why he has to go to bed, and the answer is because he has to wake up and work in the morning. She doesn't stop at five questions, and by question fifteen, he tells her, exhausted, that he has a low-paying job because he didn't study hard enough.

"Why?" she continues methodically.

"I thought partying was more fun."

Ten questions later, they're at the Big Bang and whether or not God exists.

Five is just a good cut-off point, a number by which you've likely reached the core problem without straying too far from it. I've tried it many times, both privately and at work, and it works wonders.

Example: electricity costs

We were annoyed with how much food and electricity we wasted at home. Five years after we moved into our sixty-year-old, poorly insulated, big wooden house, electricity was still our heat source. Our electricity bill for January 2011 was an appalling $1,700. We were burning money.

So we tried the "5 Whys" method on our electricity costs.

Problem	We have a huge electricity bill
Why?	We have direct electric heating in a big, old, poorly insulated wooden house.
Why?	We can't agree on installing a new heat source.
Why?	We have completely different perspectives on loans. One of us doesn't want to take out any loans at all ("he who is in debt isn't free"), while the other is willing to take out a loan if it means we can make an investment that is good for our savings and the environment in the long run.
Why?	We haven't had a proper discussion about our views on our finances; we have no dialogue about how we use resources. Therefore, sometimes we live below our means and sometimes we live beyond them.
Why?	We're avoiding this touchy subject. We have never discussed point-by-point what we wish our situation could be, and our perspectives on investments and spending are so different that they have culminated in a monthly outbreak of frustration when the bills are due.

So, belatedly, we have invested in geothermal heating and this year's January heating bill was $500 as opposed to last year's $1,700. (And the average temperature in January was not significantly different.) If we had done so when we moved in, our investment would have already paid for itself.

Example: food

Many studies show that in the Western world, we throw away an average of one-third of our food. Imagine three portions of food in front of you. One of them is thrown away. All the time. Every day. And most of it (60%) is edible when tossed in the trash. In Sweden, 900,000 tons of edible food are thrown away annually. We probably wasted more than average, partly because we served our kids too much food, and partly because we were quite wasteful with our leftovers. We didn't plan our shopping trips, so we were never sure if our produce had gone bad. On top of all that, Mattias and I both ate out for lunch, while our dinner leftovers ended up in the garbage. We didn't even compost.

In the old peasant society of Sweden, two or three generations back, people fought for every crumb. We must regain respect for ingredients when cooking meals, and we must take care of leftovers. My parents grew up in the countryside, and I regularly saw dismay flicker across their faces when we cleared our dishes from the table with half the meal left on the children's plates.

Both environmentally and in terms of our household economy, squandered food was one of the biggest wastes of resources in our home.

Problem	We throw away a lot of food
Why?	The children don't eat what's on their plates, and many organic ingredients go bad.
Why?	We serve the children their food rather than letting them help themselves, and we do a lot of impulse shopping and improvised cooking. We throw away leftovers.
Why?	We eat out at lunch and leftovers aren't eaten. We don't plan menus; rather, our meal planning is highly reactive.

Why?	We spend too much money on good ingredients, and we sincerely believe that dinner and breakfast together are incredibly important, but we don't plan for them. We lose a lot of time trying to conjure up tasty, nutritious meals that we haven't planned.
Why?	In recent years, we have needed to be more economical with our time than with our resources. As a result, we've impulse shopped for fairly expensive food, which we haven't put to good use. We lost reverence and respect for ingredients.

Today, we have cut our food costs by more than half. The rare occasions on which we throw away food now feel like a failure. Together, we save a total of $120 per week by bringing lunch to work – around $4,600 in one year. The edible food we used to throw away ends up in our lunch bags instead. Soon, we'll have saved up enough for a trip to Paris.

We serve up smaller portions and take seconds instead. We eat more seasonally, and we're smart about planning our meal streams: we have six fixed weekly menus with a prepared shopping list. We've learned to cook wisely: if we use half a bunch of basil in one dish, we plan to prepare another dish that will use up the other half, and so forth.

Part of the problem

It is far too easy for citizens to point the finger of blame at industry (and from the other side, they're pointing at consumers). In fact, industry is composed of middlemen who process something for you. Households have an incredible power and mandate for change. Take a chance, so you can hold your head high when your grandchildren ask what you did to make the planet a more sustainable place.

I once met Native American Chief Oren R. Lyons of the Onondaga Nation in New York. Oren Lyons is a professor at Buffalo University and represents the world's indigenous people in the UN. He told me that when his people make important decisions, they consider how those choices will impact their community seven generations into the future. Imagine if we were so long-sighted. Lyons emphasizes that it is equally inherent to respect all living things as it is to protect all living things. Anyone who does not believe he or she is part of the solution is always part of the problem.

Scenario: A family's dinner stream without lean

For this family of five, dinner is often the most hectic time of the day, and at the same time, it is one of the very few times during the week that they are all together. Often this time of togetherness is wasted. At 3pm, before they step into their final business meeting of the day, one of the parents is already worrying about what to serve the three children for dinner. At 4pm, they hurry to collect the children from school before dragging their hungry children to a shop to buy food for dinner. After being stuck in a traffic jam, they arrive home at 6.20pm and, too tired to cook, end up ordering pizza. By the time the pizza arrives, the children have already had a sandwich to tide them over, so one-third of the pizza is thrown away.

3.00 pm.
Anxiety at work "What are we having for dinner?" ...

3.10
SMS to partner
"Can you buy food on your way home"

No answer...

3.30
Second
SMS

4.00
Hurry to
school

4.30 At
School

8.00 pm

1/3 as food
waste on
the tip.

6.40
Pizza
delivery

6.30 Call the local fast food

6.20 At home -
to late to cook...

5.30
Traffic Jam....

nying
for the
ing

Scenario: A family's dinner stream with lean

The family now plan a menu for the week. The father took on a lot of the cooking and discovered that he had a passion for it. At least one of the children always helps him to make the dinner, which gives them quality time together. They have discovered lots of new recipes that they like, and dinnertime has become a key part of their family life.

4.30 pm. Get kids
from school

5.30

Making dinner
with the kids,
quality time.

Di
di

7.00

Leftovers
transformed
to lunchboxes

6.00

together,
tastes,
ver life.

But, returning to the home: there is another kind of waste, and it is risky and toxic. Consider a home's comprehensive stream – everything that enters the home, and everything that we create. Love, dreams, and intentions are the most important things a home contains.

Bitterness, misunderstandings, an environment where no one grows and quiet, nagging judgment are all forms of hazardous waste. And that waste can also have an influence generations down the road.

How many Earths do you need?

No matter how many Earths we'd like to have, we only get one. This is one truth that no one can repudiate and yet it is so easy to ignore. At the time we started to do lean at home, we genuinely believed we were already environmentally friendly; however, when we came to calculate our carbon footprint, we were shocked. It was a real eye opener for us.

There are several ways to calculate your own carbon footprint. One that I think is very straightforward and intuitive is the Footprint Calculator: www.footprintcalculator.org. It's easy, you simply answer questions about your accommodation, travel, eating habits, and shopping; then the calculator reveals your environmental impact and suggests ways in which you can reduce it. (You can choose to answer at two levels, either an average or add details to improve accuracy.)

The World Wide Fund (WWF) also offers a carbon footprint calculator: www.footprint.wwf.org.uk. It tells you how big your carbon footprint is and how many tonnes of CO_2 you produce per year. You will also get your impact measured against the 2020 target, as set by UK government. The WWF calculator also provides interesting facts and statistics about our effect on the planet, for instance, how one-third of all food produced is wasted, and that a year's worth of food waste in the UK represents 14 million tonnes of carbon dioxide emissions. It also says that 19 million UK homes have poor levels of energy efficiency because users are wasting energy and money heating the street around their home.

It will take you about 10–15 minutes to do this and you will be so much more aware of where your waste lies. What we realized that we started to reflect on this was how we neglect our most important needs (breathe clean air, drink clean water etc) to meet compensatory needs created by effective marketing messages.

Reducing your waste, step-by-step – *Muda*

1. Consider the areas where you have the most waste. Is it money, food, time, the environment, missed opportunities? Do you waste living space, which is often the most expensive thing we invest in, whether we're paying a mortgage or monthly rent for an apartment? Are you hard on one another's love and trust? Examine the comprehensive streams in your home, and determine where you are the most wasteful.

2. In order to address the primary causes of waste, rather than just the symptoms, you can ask the question "why" five times, which is called *Hadome*. At last, you will realize the heart of the problem, and then you can actually solve it. Naturally, it is important that you agree on what the basic problem is.

3. Lean recognizes eight types of waste: overproduction (translated to overconsumption in lean at home), lack of participation, inventory, extra work, reworking, unnecessary transportation, unnecessary waiting and unnecessary steps – for example, having to search for things. Review the eight types of waste and ask questions, such as: do we consume more than we really need? What can we stop buying? How do we share responsibility in our home (see Chapter 10)? How much time do we lose looking for things? What extra work do we do?

4. Forget your to-do list and shopping list. Replace them for a while with a stop-doing list and a get-rid-of list. On your stop-doing list, write down the things that suck up your time, but neither make you happy nor fulfill an essential need. We spend so much of our time on things that don't create any value for us or our friends and family. Write them down on a stop-doing list. A get-rid-of list can include everything from habits we want to be rid of, to old clothes and gadgets that just take up space.

5. Calculate your environmental footprint before you start implementing lean at home, then follow up later. The website for the World Wildlife Fund (WWF) has a good calculator.

6. Last but not least: make a common household budget, set savings goals and follow them up. Give the kids little cashbooks into which they can deposit and save their allowance rather than habitually spending it immediately. Pay interest!

8

KANBAN

– from reactive to proactive

What tools do you need to implement lean at home? The most common tool associated with lean is the visualization board, but all too often, lean is reduced to the visualization board alone. And that overlooks much of the point and potential of the philosophy.

Kanban means "sign" in Japanese, and we've made a lean at home *Kanban* board. It displays the puzzle that makes up our lives and includes all of our plans and everything that has to be coordinated. When the puzzle pieces of our lives were scattered everywhere – clothing hidden in piles, clutter forgotten in wardrobes, items dumped in the recycling bin when we still needed them – assembling that puzzle was a major challenge. The *Kanban* board creates a sense of predictability and expectation around what will happen. Everyone is involved in the planning, and we work together to set our priorities when there are conflicts.

Our *Kanban* board helps us keep an eye on our streams and plan how we'll meet our needs. It's our air traffic control center, and we are the officers, keeping watch and taking responsibility to prevent collisions. It's on the ground floor of our house, in the corridor between the hall and the kitchen, where the stairwell connects the top floor and the basement.

The board itself is simply a whiteboard with doors. We found it used online and bought it right away, like a small cabinet. I painted the doors a deep shade of ochre with a bronze circle. We attached pictures that make us happy to the outside of the doors, which we split into the past – the ten-year-old wedding cards, pictures from the hospital when the kids were newborns; the present – everyday candids that make us smile, travel photos and party snapshots; and the future, with pictures representing our goals – Paris, New York, mountain peaks, surfing, snowboarding, and Indian beaches. When the doors are closed, we aren't stressed by an urgent schedule. Instead, we see pictures that make us happy and remind us of what's important. At the same time, we know all the information is there, and it is liberating to feel that we have everything under control.

Predictability and expectation

When the doors are open, it's like Aladdin's cave – everything's in there. It's an annual calendar that includes major events around the world, so we know what's going on in advance, allowing us to establish context. There are birthdays, Halloween, Valentine's Day, our anniversary, International Women's Day, all of our own holidays and more: Chinese New Year, winter solstice, Ramadan, UN Day. We have something to celebrate every week.

We have an annual cycle, a circle into which we've planned seasonal variations: by when should we plant potatoes, tulip bulbs, and sunflower seeds? When will we harvest apples, potatoes, and strawberries? When should we take a dawn picnic to hear the birds? When do we fish for crayfish and lobster? When will the first mushrooms start to peek through the forest floor? It's a bit like a modern farmer's almanac. In autumn 2011, before we began using the *Kanban* board, we were all disappointed when our sunflowers froze just before opening. We had planted the seeds way too late. Our flowers struggled towards the sun along the playhouse wall for months, and just when they started to bud, the first frost hit.

Almost our entire information stream is behind those doors (not the digital variety, but we still have plenty of papers that need signing). The inside of one door has incoming documents that need to be processed in some way (paid, signed, filed). Another has documents that need to be sent on. This method lets us keep track of most of our information stream. We no longer have piles of flyers mixed in with important invoices scattered on every surface in the house, from the desk to the coffee table to the kitchen counter.

Create an overview of all of your streams. Focus on the here and now. Our whiteboard has an in-depth schedule of the next two weeks; each day has a column, and each family member has a row. We also have meal plans for the next two weeks, a row for celebrations, and a row for chores requiring more planning (Clean-o-rama, which we'll talk more about later, oiling the bikes, pruning the apple trees, and so on).

Kanban for fifteen minutes a week

Every Sunday evening, we review what's happening in the coming week. Together, we try to solve any clashes we can find, and it's so much simpler to pick, choose, and prioritize as a group. Kids want to collaborate, contribute, and feel important; you just have to find the tools to give them the opportunity to do so.

It takes ten to fifteen minutes to review what we know is coming up. We also allow for improvisation and the possibility of having friends over. We know what's going on the dinner table; we know whether anyone has anything to celebrate, and we plan out some of the group work.

While the upcoming week does have a certain predictability and expectation about it, we are careful not to squeeze in too much. We make sure everyone has a chance to rest each day, and not have to dash from one activity to the next.

The kids double-check what's going on when they have party invitations, and write down play dates themselves. It's easier for them to remember to pack their gym bags, have their piano and choir music ready, plan for field trips into the woods at school, have their baseball gloves ready for practice, and so on.

I believe that we don't become stressed and overworked because of an activity itself, but rather because of our attitude towards it, and towards the lead times and resulting lack of recovery time. With reasonable expectations, a firm grasp on the day's events, and realistic stream planning, we can enhance our ability to be fully present and enjoy ourselves.

We no longer experience the perceived lack of time that used to endlessly plague us. Successfully organizing and prioritizing our time has allowed us to enjoy our time together in a different way. Having an overview has also empowered our sense of inner control.

The same goes for our now transparent budget: we keep track of our money, and we don't live below or beyond our means. Although we have much less to spend now, we have set savings goals.

The *Kanban* board on page 72 displays everything that affects the family in any way. It shows what's going on in our comprehensive family stream. Naturally, workplace meetings aren't included, just events on evenings, weekends and so on, as well as the kids' activities. This is our joint responsibility. The board provides structure, but we are still spontaneous. It's easier to divvy up chores, and there's no single project leader. Everyone shares the same information, and we decide who will do what each Sunday evening.

A *Kanban* board can help with joint childcare planning in families where the children have two homes and spend alternate weeks with each parent. If you plan out two weeks in advance, both you and the kids will know exactly what is coming up. It will prevent that sense of a vacuum some children experience when they've packed their bags for one house or the other. It helps the parents coordinate, and gives them a better overview of what's happening in their children's lives, even during the week the house is empty. It provides the children with stability.

Information overflow

Before we started using *Kanban*, our information stream was a constant flood of everything from field trips requiring a brown-bag lunch and new mortgage applications, to the tax authorities' request for income information. Every day, homes handle an overflow of information, a stream that includes processing, decisions, documentation, signatures, and forwarding. We were not "just in time" at all in this arena, and the reminders we regularly found in our mailbox were a clear indication that we caused extra work for many authorities and organizations. Our information stream bore striking similarities to our clothing stream. It was based on a spontaneous, disorganized pile system, which meant that we managed to lose or forget important papers and bills, occasionally even tossing them out in the recycling. We received five or six letters in the mail each day, not to mention the emails we received in our joint account about various games, parties, concerts, activities, and so forth. We had no stream for this process. We didn't know if one of us had responded to an invitation; we didn't know if the bills were paid; in fact, we didn't even know if we had received a bill,-because bills could be anywhere from the mantle to the dining room table or in the workroom (which, in spring 2011, was most reminiscent of a massive, unsorted records office). Mattias had an ongoing project in which he bravely sorted ten or so piles from the workroom floor, after which I came in and absentmindedly put everything in one pile, whereupon he started over. Sisyphus and his boulder. Our home was full of unspoken systems. We never communicated them to one another, and it was chaotic and counterproductive.

Scenario: A family's information stream with lean

When a party invitation arrives from a school friend of the son, the family notes the party time on the *Kanban* screen. The boy enjoys choosing a gift for his close friend and is filled with excitement at the thought of spending an afternoon with his friends.

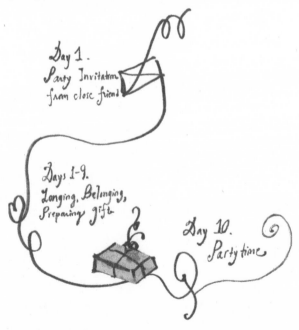

Day 1.
Party Invitation

Lost in
a paper
pile

Day 2.
Lost in
recycling

Days 4-8
Sadness,
alien-
ation

Day 3.
Party
Discussions
at school

Day 5.
Searching?... .

unused gift wrap

Day 10. Disappointed ,

All friends
at party....

Day 9.
Can you come?....

Here is an example of our *Kanban* board in February

Day	Monday	Tuesday	Wednesday	Thursday	Friday	Saturday	Sunday
Eva	Opera		Triathlon training	Stockholm evening meeting		Meetings in Nyköping	Nyköping
Mattias	Hockey			Daycare meeting		Nyköping	Soccer
Vendela	Ice skating	Gym	Going to Emily's		Emma coming over	Choir Piano Nyköping	Nyköping
Tuva	Forest field trip	Gym Lina coming over	Skating rink	Baseball Going to Clara's		Noel's party Nyköping	Soccer Nyköping
Samuel	Bring 3 pieces of fruit to school Swimming with Leo				Masquerade	Nyköping	Nyköping
Food	Thai salmon	Lentil soup	Pasta Pomodoro	Burgers	Fish stew	Brunch out	Coq au vin
Celebrate		Mardi Gras			Anniversary		
Chores			Grocery shopping	Clean-o-rama	Cleaning service		*Kanban* Meeting
Rest					Friday family night		

Creating visual management and planning, step-by-step – *Kanban*

1. Do you know what's going on in your family members' lives? Is everyone aware of everyone else's plans? Do you solve conflicts and choose what to prioritize together? Are you proactive, so that you have time to plan carpools and give other kids lifts?

2. Make sure to have a common management and planning method for everything that affects the family, preferably something visible that the children can approach, read, and add to. This method will give you a shared picture of what is in the pipeline.

3. Can you see any planning bottlenecks? Aim for a steady stream of work, and stay on top of it so that you have time to rest. When conflicts arise despite your best efforts, be proactive: choose what to prioritize and solve the problem. Carpool and invite others along more than you currently do; it's a concrete way to contribute to a more sustainable society.

4. Does one person in your family tend to feel responsible for leading all projects – everything from packing gym bags to helping out with school picnics? Why is this the case? *Kanban* offers every opportunity for joint responsibility.

5. Do you have an overview of the (perhaps overflowing) information stream in your home? Make a *Kanban* board and have a once-weekly, fifteen-minute meeting.

6. Are you aware of current events? Do you have a general understanding of what's going on in society and the world, so that you can establish a sense of security and predictability about what the media reports? Write down events on the calendar, everything from elections in the UK and the Cannes Film Festival to the World Series and Nobel festivities.

整理

9

SEIRI

– from chaos to calm

Never sweep anything under the rug – in lean, that is a sacred concept. Problems will just slide back out to be solved. A lean leader once said that to see problems, you have to clean everywhere. An oil stain on the floor means something is not working properly, so don't just clean it up: ask yourself why it is there at all. When guests from the West visited Japanese factories in the 1970s and '80s, they were always surprised by the level of cleanliness, often saying they could practically eat off the floor. Eating off the floor at our house couldn't be done without risking a bacterial infection.

To eliminate different kinds of waste that lead to mistakes, defects, and maybe even injuries, Japan has the 5S program. It is a way to achieve and maintain order and tidiness. 5S stands for *Seiri* (sort, clear out), *Seiton* (structure), *Seiso* (shine, clean), *Seiketsu* (standardize), and *Shitsuke* (sustain, create a habit).

5S – definitions

1. **SEIKETSU** – standardize. Create rules to establish permanence for the first "S". We agreed that the best way to manage annoying tasks was to do them immediately. For example, we always make our beds in the morning, and we always sweep under the dining-room table and load the dishwasher right after a meal. Lastly, if you stop all the debate, you will do things automatically. Keeping a beautiful broom near the dinner table makes it easy to sweep away crumbs without a second thought. Considering how many decisions you make every day, it frees up a great deal of energy to get rid of a few unnecessary ones that only cause negativity.

2. **SEIRI** – sort through your seldom-used items and clear them out. The average consumer wears 20% of all the clothing they own. Donate and sell the clothes you don't wear, or reuse the fabric to make something new. Examine everything you own that occupies living space and sucks up energy. Sort it out and keep only what you truly need or love. It doesn't matter how many brilliant storage systems you have if your home is flooded with things you never use.

3. **SEITON** – while clearing things out, structure what is left. Organize your belongings, choose a place for everything, then keep everything in its place. I believe that in our era of consumption, messes of gizmos and gadgets make it hard to live functional lives at home (just think of all the overloaded kids' rooms you've seen). Ultimately, that can lower quality of life. Imagine the time you could save if you didn't have to search for things, the energy you wouldn't waste feeling irritated. It only takes a fraction of that time to decide and describe where things will belong.

4. **SEISO** – shine, clean: order makes everything significantly easier. Decide what should be done when cleaning. If you detest dusting, vacuuming, or scrubbing the floors, think of a way to make it less of a drag. Why not listen to an entertaining audiobook that you only get to listen to while clea-

ning? Or, perhaps cleaning could be the only time you let yourself eat your favorite chocolate.

5. **SHITSUKE** – sustain by creating a habit. Remember, it's almost as easy to create a good habit as it is to create a bad one. For example, try keeping the soap on a small sponge in the bathroom, making it easy to give the sink a quick wipe whenever you want. No chemicals, just a little bit of soap.

Fine and festive

We created our own variation of 5S: we implemented Clean-o-rama, inspired by our kids' school. Clean-o-rama takes place each Thursday, and it's an honored tradition in our family. This is how it all began:

Every other month, Vendela and Tuva receive a pretty invitation from their school:

Clean-o-rama!

Our school will be hosting Clean-o-rama on Thursday, February 23. We will clear up and clean out each and every room from top to bottom. Once we're done, we will celebrate with tons of tasty exotic treats.

Everyone is welcome to bring two exotic fruits for a potluck. We will have a beautiful spread to enjoy together!

During Clean-o-rama, the kids are responsible for cleaning the class-rooms, craft room, science room, and so forth. Each room has a set of cleaning instructions to be checked off. The teacher, named Åsa, ins-pects the rooms afterwards. It's a festive day at school, and the chil-dren look forward to it. Woe to the parent who comes to pick anyone up early on that day! Clean-o-rama is predictable, and when it's over, everything looks beautiful and the kids celebrate with a party.

We have indulged in a cleaning service for our house every other week, and they clean all the floors, the kitchen, laundry room, and kids' rooms. Before we started lean at home, the evening before the cleaners came was an absolute nightmare. We tried to pick up to give them a fighting chance of actually cleaning, still shoveling piles of stuff into drawers and wardrobes well after midnight. After the ser-vice, our house was certainly spick and span, but our belongings were hidden willy-nilly in various storage areas, and we ended up spending hours looking for them.

Quite simply, it was a total waste.

A lightbulb moment

One evening in September, when Mattias was at a conference and the kids and I sat eating dinner, I suddenly remembered that the cleaning service was coming the next day. I looked around in despair, taking in everything that needed to be moved, and let out a heavy sigh.

Vendela, our oldest daughter, read my mind, and said happily, "We can have Clean-o-rama!"

Abracadabra: creativity erupted, with instructions written up for every room and Clean-o-rama signs drawn and posted. Tuva volunteered to play the role of Åsa, the teacher, inspecting each space to make sure everything was done properly.

So now we have a routine, a clear expectation of what has to be done, and then we celebrate (usually with ice cream). It takes about two hours for everyone to clear up the house to the rhythm of upbeat music sounding from the speakers. We no longer panic before the cleaning service comes.

Our Clean-o-rama routine

This is our Clean-o-rama routine. Each room has a specific set of instructions, but generally speaking:

» We dust.

» We put things away.

» We change the sheets.

» We take out all the recycling to the recycling center.

» We sort out the Clean-o-rama box (a box that was once never emptied and clogged with everything but the kitchen sink, that is now a place for homeless items that we don't know whether to save, or where they should go. During Clean-o-rama, we sort through it and decide what to give away and what to keep).

Clean-o-rama combines four of the five S's: *Seiri* – sort and clear out, *Seiso* – shine, clean, *Seiketsu* – standardize, and *Shitsuke* – sustain by creating a habit.

Need or love

Seiton, or structure, is not part of Clean-o-rama. Instead, we work with *Seiton* in the context of creating streams: for example, when reviewing the clothing stream, structure comes in when we decide where to store each garment, and so on. An important difference exists between classic organization and lean. Your wardrobe may be perfectly organized, filled with clean, ironed clothes and beautifully arranged by color. But considering that about 80% of clothing is never worn, you might suffer from suboptimization.

Lean thinking is not just about hanging everything up. You have to consider the entire thread – the total stream – from shopping to giving the garment away.

When asked how to clear clutter from the home, English organization guru Terence Conran responded, "Pull every single thing out of your home, and spread it all out on a big tarp. Only save the things you absolutely need or love."

This advice is undeniably drastic, but we've tried to follow it. Suddenly, we were able to start using the workroom; we turned our dressing room into a children's room; we emptied the piles of toys out of the playroom in the basement and had space to move in a ping-pong table.

Considering how much stuff is both loved and needed, you may as well get rid of everything else. And above all, be sure to keep unnecessary things from entering your home from the start. We once had a very calm, analytical friend over to visit. Her little girl loved a soft doll we had, and wished for one for her birthday. Her mother responded, "We'll see if she can move in with us." What a beautiful choice of words: something moves in, rather than being acquired. It gives you a different perspective.

Getting rid of things you never use is not wasteful. But still, maybe you think you might be able to use some of these objects in the future. Consider this perspective instead: it wastes space and energy to save such things, and to continue taking care of them. In late 2010, a few of our close relatives passed away. Our family inherited some objects and paintings that I knew meant a lot to my relatives, things that had been in our family for a long time. We kept these things for a year, and then we began giving away what we couldn't take care of. Every time, we had to remind ourselves that we weren't betraying the family: we treasure our memories of relatives who have passed on, not their things.

Many people also probably buy into the myth that clutter and chaos are par for the course in a family with young children, that they're just part of raising kids. One way to motivate yourself to get the mess under control is to begin timing how long it takes to look for things amidst the clutter. More than likely, you will realize that no longer having to search for things all the time will quickly earn back your invested time.

We timed the searches at our house for a few weeks and found that on average, the five of us spent a total of around 700 minutes weekly searching for things that had disappeared. Too often, those searches ended with never finding what we were looking for, and buying duplicates or even triplicates. Today, we spend a maximum total of 70 minutes each week looking for things (distributed among five people, that's about 15 minutes a week).

Overpriced living space

Visit each room and look around: what role does this room play? What items do you absolutely need and truly love that help the room meet its function? Why are other things here? Where should they go?

And then, get rid of stuff! Because no matter how big or small your living space is, whether you live in a rented apartment or your own house, you're paying a surcharge for living space if you fill it up with meaningless clutter.

Our family realized just how many things we saved, all of which were exposed during this process. These weren't things we particularly enjoyed seeing or used daily; it was simply stuff that we shuffled from place to place. Here are a few principles we try to hold ourselves to when it comes to *Seiton* (structure).

» We keep the floor clear.

» We decide where to keep things, and we have labels inside drawers and cupboard doors.

» The things we choose to keep front and center are things we either enjoy or things we use daily. Naturally, it is ideal if these things meet both criteria. We moved unfinished projects-in-progress to the garage so that we don't have constant reminders of incomplete tasks.

» In the kitchen, dining room, living room, TV room, bathroom and hallways – the spaces everyone shares – we've agreed on certain rules, and we stick to them. We use the eminent Montessori nursery rule: you always put a toy away when you take out something else. And it's not just toys; we grown-ups are also trying to learn to put things back where they belong.

Organization and tidiness, step-by-step – 5S

1. Enter a room and think about what function the room serves. Then consider each item in the room: what do you truly need? What has sentimental value? Only save the things you either love or really need.

2. How much does all the unnecessary stuff in your home cost in rent each year? Given that urban living space in particular is often the most expensive thing we invest in, you're essentially paying a surcharge at home if you have any space you don't use because it's filled with stuff. Calculate how much living space unnecessary stuff takes up, and how much that space is worth.

3. Think from a climate perspective, too: how much space is unnecessarily heated?

These first three steps culminate in *Seiri* – sort and purge

4. How much time do you spend looking for things? How many things that don't have a place are shuffled around your home? Make a top-ten list of the things you most often have to look for.

5. Organize your belongings. Choose a place for everything. It's ridiculously simple: attach little labels that say what each space should hold. No item should be homeless.

This process results in *Seiton* – structure

6 **Implement Clean-o-rama!** Make it an honored tradition. Everyone helps clean all the rooms. You will have already decided what should be done in every room, and when you're done, you get to celebrate.

At Clean-o-rama, you sort and clear out (Seiri), clean (*Seiso*), you standardize (*Seiketsu*), and you create a habit (*Shitsuke*).

10

HANSEI

– from regret to reflection

When Toyota Motor Corporation was established just before World War II broke out, the management likened the new company to a delicate, freshly planted tree. They were inexperienced and thus quite conservative; they never made rash decisions. They asked questions like, "What do we believe makes a tree beautiful? What does not? What decisions have we made today to help this tree grow a little stronger, a little more beautiful?"

How often have you asked the questions: what is a good home to me? What is not a good home? What have I done today to make my daily life a little better?

Hansei can be translated as "reflection." In Japanese culture, learning and taking responsibility are key, and many consider Toyota to be one of the best learning organizations around. Lean at home is about reflecting on what you and your family consider to be a good home, and evaluating how your home meets everyone's needs. It's also about monitoring, looking back, and learning from what's gone well and what hasn't. In addition, look ahead to determine how you will realize your goals and dreams.

What is a good home to you?

Do you want your home to be a place of rest, given that most of your life unfolds outside it? Should it convey joy, energy, and hopefulness? Should it be an open, welcoming home that nurtures relationships and encourages a sense of community? A place for continuous learning and exploration, a creative environment? A status symbol, something that strengthens your personal brand? A place where everyone evolves and achieves their dreams and self-actualization? A playground paradise with blissful kids, few rules and procedures, where the adults stand back? A place that shuts out the world, where you can be in your own safe haven? Or where you absorb the outside world, discuss it, relate to it? An improvement project, an investment to continue your residential career and crown it with a high-status living space?

Think about what you want your home to be, but also, think about what you don't want it to be. Recently, a figure fluttered past as I read the morning paper: 40% of parents of young children renovate their houses. Why? Is it an optimal time in their lives? What role does marketing play, or all of those design shows pushing a dream image of how a home should look?

In many homes, the people sharing a roof have completely different ideas about what makes a good home and how it should function. I once had a colleague who always returned to work on Mondays feeling exhausted. His wife loved having friends over at the weekend – close friends and relatives visited them regularly – but all he wanted was to take the boat out on the lake with his sons. When I asked him whether he had expressed this to his wife, he looked at me inquisitively and said he believed she should understand already. They had carried on that way for a decade.

Another friend was wholly responsible for her home when her children were young. She spent her weekdays caring for the home, and craved a getaway by the time Saturday rolled around. Meanwhile, her partner wanted nothing more than to relax in their perfect home at the weekends – it was a space that she struggled to maintain, but that began to feel like a prison.

Not daydreams

Think about what you consider a good day, and about what you want to cultivate and achieve. Then look back, reflect, and learn from the past.

If you don't think about your long-term goals and the trajectory of your life, you may end up resorting to short-term, counterproductive actions, and only meeting compensatory needs. Differentiate between daydreams and what you truly want – recognize the dreams you can actually achieve with courage, perseverance, and an action plan, and recognize which dreams your home can help you achieve. This is essential.

We wrote down our long-term goals, and what we consider a good home. We wanted our home to be open and welcoming, a place where we could all grow at our own pace. We wanted a home that conveyed joy and creativity, and that always had room for one more plate at the dinner table.

We wanted a more peaceful dinner table. Our mealtimes were fun, but they were also noisy and rushed. Our family's table manners left much to be desired. In retrospect, I think our dinner-table situation was a mirror image of our family.

We wanted to defend ourselves against celebrity idolization and pass on some true historic heroes to our children. We decided to make a portrait wall, which was inspired by our visit to Thomas Jefferson's library in Virginia. Today, our wall features brave, bright people ranging from Martin Luther King to Malala.

Reflect on the present

Before you start thinking about your dreams, it is important to make sure you are meeting your most basic needs. Because if we look at the home as a gigantic needs factory, and if we are committed to continuously trying to meet needs in the here and now, we must focus on the most essential needs first – those that simply cannot be deprioritized. The fact of the matter is that you can only strive for self-actualization if and when you have met your basic needs.

This is where *Hansei* (reflection) comes in, and a tool we can use to help with this process is Maslow's Hierarchy of Needs (named after American psychologist Abraham Maslow), a classic model. Checking off points in the hierarchy of needs will allow you to confirm whether the needs of each family member are being met, or if one individual is sacrificing his or her own needs in order to meet the needs of others. Reflecting on Maslow's hierarchy of needs will shed light on the situation, whether it is happening knowingly or not. Maslow listed five levels of needs:

What are you living on, who are you living with, and what are you living for?

In your home, your everyday life, you need to meet some of the most basic needs, so the question is, are you meeting your survival needs or are you focusing on secondary needs? Consider how you meet the most basic needs, such as clean air, water, sleep, healthy food. Are these sacrificed for something else? Does everyone in your home meet their most basic needs, and make time for self-care? Take time to reflect on these questions.

1. **PHYSIOLOGICAL NEEDS** such as food, water, sleep, oxygen, and warmth. Simply put, these are the most basic needs. They can control our thoughts and behavior as long as they aren't being satisfied, because our focus is on survival.

2. **SAFETY NEEDS**, i.e. psychological needs like peace, stability, structure, security, and protection. Where unpredictable chaos may have once existed, lean at home helps give structure to life.

3. **NEED FOR LOVE AND BELONGING** – social needs, such as love, friendship, connection, understanding, and acceptance. We have an intense need to feel needed and understood, for communal belonging and participation, for love. We live longer, happier lives by attaining these things.

These three levels are considered deficiency needs, and the next two levels are growth needs. If the deficiency needs go unmet, it is difficult to meet the growth needs. As a matter of course, the home must fulfill the three deficiency needs for all family members. Shortcomings here entail consequences for life in general. Thoroughly analysing how the home meets these needs is an important part of lean at home. The first level, physiological needs – such as oxygen and water – are directly linked to whether we manage to live more sustainably in society, so that we do not destroy our local environment. Everything is interrelated. If someone's basic needs are not being met, that must lead to a change. Fast.

4. **NEED FOR RESPECT AND SELF-ESTEEM** – ego needs, such as self-respect, recognition, attention and acknowledgment. It's easy to become unbalanced here – consider how much recognition and acknowledgment you receive at work relative to how much you receive for the work you do at home. Where do you or your partner choose to spend your time and energy? It can easily become a downward spiral, with one of you progressively abdicating from the home. A person who feels valuable at work but worthless at home may be slowly wandering out of the door. One day, he or she may not come back.

5. **NEED FOR SELF-ACTUALIZATION** – to evolve as a person and reach your full potential. If you have met all of your other needs, you can devote yourself to self-development and self-realization, to blossoming. Some people find that this happens after a divorce – they suddenly have time for self-actualization. It is a shame that they did not get, or take, that time earlier.

After Maslow

Once you've reviewed how your home meets these needs (hopefully, you will find that you are indeed meeting the basic needs), you can hammer out self-actualization goals and ways to achieve them in daily life. In business, target documents typically contain basic targets and growth targets, which are usually followed up twice a year. That same tactic can also be used for all family members at home to track and encourage everyone's growth, and to make sure everyone's basic needs are being met. This way, no individual will sacrifice himself or herself for the others. So consider how you meet basic needs, and the opportunities everyone has for self-actualization.

Like most parents of young children, we realized we could be drastically better at appreciating and acknowledging one another's efforts. We also needed to give each other space for self-actualization. Reviewing Maslow's needs, it became clear that we were sacrificing our basic needs for sleep and exercise for other needs. Eight years of caring for young children had left their mark: a deep web of wrinkles had formed beneath my eyes, and my sleep deficit was enormous. I began occasionally sleeping in the basement guest room, which increased my number of nights slept all the way through by about 50%.

We have also eliminated the bottlenecks that were preventing us from exercising. Mattias runs to work at least twice weekly, and he cycles the rest of the time. I've become almost as dependent on my running shoes as my lipstick.

Break the silent tyranny

Reflection leads to genuine learning, so look back and learn from what you have done – the things that went well, and the things that didn't. What form do reflection and follow-up take for you?

Do you have a quiet voice in your mind that criticizes how everything works – or doesn't work – at home? A nagging, negative monologue spouting off everything that irritates you? A pessimistic whisper that becomes a reality? Or does that judgment come out as a bitter fight? Don't plant roots in sour soil.

In the wonderful book *Family construction – the blueprint to help you understand and build a family*, family counselor Madeleine Cocozza writes:

> *People judge their families continuously in the back of their minds, talking to themselves and evaluating quietly. It may turn out okay; in the grand scheme of things, they may be satisfied with their families and their conditions. But those judgments can also stir a deep sense of dissatisfaction. Discussing dissatisfaction can be challenging, but if unshared with your partner, that emotion might fester [...] Serious dissatisfaction in a relationship must be eliminated to preserve family life.*

With or without lean at home, honest follow-up is essential. But in terms of lean, if you don't follow up your efforts honestly, then your changes won't be lasting. You won't successfully have continuous improvements, and you won't achieve your goals.

This isn't about confrontation; it's about reflecting together on where you're heading and how your journey is progressing. Acknowledge and celebrate the things that have gone well, and think about what has not and what you can do to improve. Never let a bitter, brutal silence hover like a storm cloud over your home.

Shift your focus: rather than accusing your partner of not doing something, acknowledge and appreciate everything that has indeed been accomplished. Let's return again to our metaphor: if creating a home is planting a tree, what have we done and what decisions have we made to make the tree more beautiful? What choices have we made that have not made the tree more beautiful? What can we learn from those experiences to make the tree stronger and lovelier tomorrow?

Learning instead of wasting

In lean, mistakes are seen as a chance to learn. Today it is considered high praise indeed for a company to be recognized as a learning organization. American researcher Peter Senge made the concept famous in his book *The Fifth Discipline*, which defines learning organizations as places "where people continually expand their capacity to create the results they truly desire, where new and expansive patterns of thinking are nurtured, where collective aspiration is set free, and where people are continually learning how to learn together."

That is why I believe it is so valuable to evaluate continuously: so that you can see where you are going. Introspection, rather than accusations against one another, should form the foundation of your evaluation. Happiness often means being on your way, on the right track, yearning for and feeling that we are moving in the same direction. And it is undeniably easier to change oneself than it is to change someone else.

You must decide yourselves how often to hold evaluations and how to carry them out. But perhaps most important of all is to consider the present: how do you currently carry out evaluations? Even if at first glance you think you aren't making them, you are. Judging might manifest as an inner voice, or it might take the form of arguments and angry accusations.

Blow-ups over bills

In spring 2011, our evaluations took the form of a parody and comprised two classic scenes. One played out monthly, when it was time to pay the bills, and the other every evening, when it was time to run the dishwasher. We were often both completely exhausted and longing for just one thing: sleep.

We had no budget, and we had never discussed our diametrically opposed views of loans in any detail. The bills always came as a nasty shock. Once a month, the day after pay day and the day before the bills were to be paid, we had our ritual bill night. Since we both knew what would play out, we did everything to delay that ceremony on the bank's website. Finally, as the clock approached midnight the night before the mortgage would be deducted from our account, we would begin a frenzied hunt for bills.

After finding embarrassing late notices in the midst of our paper piles, step two would begin: while kicking at an old bureau, I would angrily question the purchases my husband had made, purchases I thought were fun surprises just days before. Mattias (who is the accepting sort) would smirk at my comical appearance, which only frustrated me more – I never said anything vicious, I just ranted like a poorly media-trained politician about the same things as the month before, and the year before...a long, self-important monologue about my thriftiness and his genuine status as a shopaholic. At last, through sweat and tears, the invoices would all be paid, and our hard-earned wages would slip away like sand in an hourglass.

Mattias and I approach shopping differently. He thinks it's fun to make intelligent purchases, while I am gripped by Lutheran guilt whenever I enter a store. I try to get the whole thing over with as quickly as possible, which means I often go home with fairly pricey purchases.

In our family, we had an unspoken agreement that Mattias was the buyer. But because I was so indifferent to the purchasing process that resulted in our treasures, I was shocked every time I saw our expenses.

To be sure, we were not particularly constructive with our use of financial resources. Our electric bills were always the heftiest: Sweden was in the grips of a particularly biting winter, and we practically paid for a trip to Thailand for two each month.

Dishes in the dishwasher formed our other classic conflict. If I filled the dishwasher, Mattias would usually sneak in and rearrange everything. He had patiently tried to explain to me the best way to fill the machine, but I never really took interest, and I didn't listen well.

Integrity and cooperation

Since we began monitoring the actual causes of frustration, we have both made an effort to change – that is, to change ourselves – and we've listened to and learned from one another.

We have a budget and we discuss all major purchases. We borrow tools from friends, and we lend out our things in exchange. We consider where we can renovate, and what we should absolutely give up.

It took me five minutes to listen to Mattias and learn the best dishwasher loading method. We no longer end up with ugly chipped cups, poorly washed silverware, or knocked-over glasses that have to be rewashed. We do things right from the start, and it's so wonderfully simple. This is pure *Kaizen*.

What would it clearly be useful for you to agree upon at home? Where we once had different ways of solving problems, we now find a happy middle ground that we can both agree upon. For example, we defined what we mean by "cleaning up" after a meal. In my world, you wipe the dining-room table to a sheen, sweep under the table, wipe down the sink and put everything away. In Mattias' world, you clear the dining-room table, rinse the dishes and pop them in the dishwasher, perhaps leaving the casserole dish that needs to be washed by hand. Today, we compromise.

So it's pretty simple. Agree on what you will do and how it will be done, then check that you've done it.

Naturally, this approach is built on integrity and cooperation. It is just as important to listen to yourself as it is to listen to your partner, to be able to trust that yes means yes, and the other person can count on it. In the long-term, constantly sacrificing yourself for others entails major challenges to family cohesion. Martyrdom has no place in the modern family.

Beginning to reflect, step-by-step – *Hansei*

Reflecting on the future

1. Reflect on and describe what you consider a good home and what you do not consider a good home. Lean is a dynamic way of life that is characterized by continuous improvements. It isn't static.

2. Ask each other questions about the goals and dreams your home can help fulfill. Your home is the one place on earth that you can have the most impact, so do it. What is a beautiful tree to you?

3. Lean is a way to continually grow. Our closest relationships help us evolve the most, but they are also where we run the biggest risk of getting stuck, coming to a standstill, and forgetting what we really want.

4. Lean is a way to continually evolve, learn lessons, and gain greater knowledge, experience and understanding of needs and how they change over time. We create a home in which we are prepared for life's different phases.

Reflect on the present

1. Do you have a balanced method for meeting the needs of each family member? Using Maslow's hierarchy of needs (*see* page 86), review how your whole family's needs are met, including parents and children.

2. If you do not meet Maslow's three basic needs, it will be hard to achieve the upper levels: self-actualization and self-esteem. If they are unfulfilled, focus all of your efforts on fulfilling the three survival needs.

Reflecting on the past

1. What kind of judgments do you make at home? Do you have a quiet inner critic? Do you have a dialogue? Even if at first glance you think you aren't making judgments, a quiet voice that may be unspoken, or may be aggressive and noisy, is indeed there.

2. Be sure to set aside time for follow-up. Don't forget to ask questions, such as: what have we done well? Have we spent our energy on things that are important to us? What have we done to achieve our goals and create a home that is good for us?

3. How do you view mistakes at home? As failures, or as learning opportunities? Reflection (*Hansei*) and continuous improvements (*Kaizen*) help turn a home into a learning organization.

11

MURA AND MURI

– from running the house to sharing the load

Participation and respect for people are key components of lean. Think about how you distribute tasks: do you put everyone's creative energy to use? It may seem obvious, but it's worth repeating: the key to smooth leadership – parenting – is for both adults to be happy with their parenting model. It is just like in business: if some leaders in your management group aren't on board and feel dissatisfied with how things are progressing, the company will never take off. That situation will send mixed messages to your organization.

Two things are required for a lean home: love and intention. Both adults should think lean at home is a good idea in order for it to be successful (although one person may be more excited than the other). The intention has to be there.

Even workloads and putting everyone's creativity to use are also key pieces of lean culture. Earlier, we talked about *Muda* – that which is not value-creating, i.e. waste. But there are two other "M"s that are just as important for lean to work: **Muri** and **Mura**. People should not be overburdened (*Muri*) nor have vastly uneven streams (*Mura*).

Whether consciously or unconsciously, a number of organizations have grossly misinterpreted or manipulated lean, giving it a bad reputation in some circles. These organizations seem to think lean is about an insane amount of streamlining, overburdening employees, and reducing staff. It should be the opposite: it's impossible to have a lean culture if your staff is overburdened, which more and more companies are realizing.

The tortoise and the hare

A legendary lean leader, Taiichi Ohno, said, "The slow but consistent tortoise causes less waste and is much preferred over the speedy hare, who rushes off only to have to stop and rest."

No one should feel overburdened or have an inconsistent amount of work. Nor should anyone have to rush to finish countless tasks one minute, but have nothing to do the next. Avoid what takes place in some hospitals: planning a steady stream of work at far too high a pace, with constant overcrowding and employees who don't even have time to go to the bathroom.

Establish regularity and predictability – be slow and steady like the tortoise, not fast and inconsistent like the hare. What do you do at home? Are you always dashing from one chore to the next, still covered in soap, rather than being present and methodical with what you do?

Business and politics always involve discussions about how leadership is shared. Do we do that in the family? Or does one person take on more responsibility? Have we developed a habit of supporting and helping others, and is that effort acknowledged? How many times have you seen women assume that role, both at home and in the public sphere: a woman on a corporate executive management team who covers up the CEO's every gaffe? A woman who never takes center stage herself, only polishes it for the highest exec?

That role must be dropped from the family. Shared responsibility must be required of both partners, emotionally, financially, and practically. Protecting your own integrity is not selfish, but if caring for others is taken too far, you may feel guilty when they take care of themselves. And that's a problem for the entire home.

Sheets of white paper

Danish family therapist Jesper Juul often talks about the interplay between parents that indicates the atmosphere in the home. Obviously, the practical and emotional sides of being a good parent must be discussed and shared. Shirking responsibility is inconsistent with a desire to be a lifelong good parent. It is awful to feel that you've been taken advantage of, and that feeling is a direct threat to the atmosphere of the home.

Try the following exercise: each of you should have your own sheet of white paper in front of you. Draw two or three columns, with one column for each adult. If you have children, label one column for the kids. The first column is yours: mark the percentage of chores you believe you do, and what they are. The second column is your perception of your partner: mark how much and what you believe he or she does. In the third column, do the same for the children. Your partner should do the same. If your kids are old enough, they can join in and draw columns indicating how much of the total housework they believe they do.

This is one lens through which to view your parenting, and a way to estimate the distribution of responsibility.

If both parents work full-time, then ideally, the columns should be the same size. When you complete this exercise, it is important to truly consider everything you do at home, including social, emotional, practical, and financial work.

This exercise is about perception, appreciation, and acknowledgment.

Label your column with what you do and how much time it takes. The next step, which may be amusing or may be worrisome, is to compare your estimate to your partner's. There are so many things that one partner does that the other may be completely unaware of, and vice versa. Things only become apparent when they are not done.

It is incredibly easy to do. Write down everything, and I mean everything, big and small. Don't be sloppy and don't forget anything – that is key. Everything counts, from charging the lawnmower battery to buying new gym shoes for the kids, from wiping the crumbs off the dining-room table to driving the kids to their activities.

Gender equality

In spring 2011, work allocation in our home was exceptionally lop-sided. That was likely to do with the huge amount of stress I faced at my job, where many employees were overburdened and hitting the wall. My workplace problems were invading our home sphere. Sound familiar?

Those problems affected Mattias. He ended up in the part-time trap, working 36 hours a week, but shouldering 75–80% of the responsibility at home. As a result of a 10% reduction in working hours, he ended up responsible for nearly everything at home. We also saw that the kids' column was way too low; we could definitely have more participation from them. They wanted to pitch in; we just had to find smart ways for them to do so.

Today we share the chores equally, and the kids do about 10%. They clean their rooms, help cook and clean up after meals, put away what they take out, put their clothes in the dirty laundry, fold their clothes, and are largely responsible for their own hygiene (with our help). The Italian doctor and child development specialist Maria Montessori's words sometimes fade away when my first impulse is to step in and do something to speed things up: "any unnecessary help is a hindrance to the child's development."

It makes sense to start thinking this way when the kids are young, to allow them to participate even if their contributions occasionally hinder more than help. Laying the groundwork for taking responsibility when they're young is important, because otherwise, how can you expect them to do so when they're teenagers?

This simple sketch of columns is a powerful tool to change work distribution, and perhaps make it a little more equal.

Increasing participation, step-by-step – *Mura* and *Muri*

1. Estimate your distribution of responsibility: sit down with a sheet of white paper in front of each of you, and draw two or three columns. In the first column, mark the percentage of chores you believe you do, and what they are. In the second column, mark how much and what you believe your partner does.

2. Your partner should do the same. If you have kids, include a column for your child/children.

3. Next, compare your columns. This is a starting point for change and a way to generate participation and acknowledgment of everyone's efforts. Make the invisible visible – don't just highlight when something is not done.

4. Exchange columns, or rewrite your gender contract at home: try exchanging tasks so that you don't keep doing what you've always done, or what your parents always did.

5. Make sure to genuinely understand, appreciate, and acknowledge one another's efforts. Consider how much feedback you (hopefully) give and receive at work – try doing that at home, too.

12

ONE YEAR OF LEAN LIVING: THE RESULTS

– how our home was transformed by lean (though our journey has only just begun)

After systematically working with lean, our results show that lean at home truly holds an enormous power for change. It is a philosophy and a cohesive system that takes a holistic approach, in which we work together to find lasting changes that create participation. And our journey has only just begun.

We are realizing our dreams, and our children's. We have cut costs in half – without sacrificing quality of life. We still live in our house – but we've invested in streams, reducing our impact on the environment, and using fewer resources. We're training for a marathon and a triathlon; before, we didn't exercise at all. We're eating better and more healthily, and we barely ever throw food away anymore.

We have reviewed how we meet all the needs of our home, and we've made changes to make things run smoothly and eliminate bottlenecks that create frustration. For example, the laundry stream is ten times faster, and we have got rid of all the piles of clothes that used to be everywhere in the house (these days, we even iron our clothes once in a while).

We don't spend hours looking for anything that has been hidden, forgotten, or emptied somewhere (hairbrushes, invitations, reflectors, clothes, the garlic press, bills, and so on). We have reduced the time we once spent looking for things from a total of about 700 minutes a week to 70 minutes. We no longer end searches by buying duplicates and triplicates of everything from spices to mittens – in general, we can find what we're looking for.

Today, we usually recognize when we are doing extra work right away – because remember, the awful thing about extra work is that you often think you're doing something value-creating, when in fact you've missed meeting the actual, primary need; for instance, like when we had to clear the garden of fallen fruit the autumn before last, because we didn't harvest the apples in time (sadly, a waste of both time and many lovely apples).

Environmental footprint

We've started making changes and we've continued implementing continuous improvements. We discuss our goals and follow them up; we no longer have an ongoing quiet, critical monologue, that seed of dissatisfaction. We acknowledge one another's work, and the kids take more responsibility for chores at home.

We waste less food and we waste less energy. For example, we saved at least $4,600 in one year by taking lunch to work. Sometimes we treat ourselves to a leisurely lunch with friends and colleagues – and when we do, we really enjoy it – rather than burning fifteen dollars a day on an unhealthy pasta dish.

Using the World Wildlife Fund's (WWF's) calculator, we've calculated our past and present environmental footprint, and the difference is dramatic. Before, our joint annual carbon dioxide emissions totaled 25.8 tons. If everyone lived as we were living, we would need more than eight planets. That footprint doesn't even include air travel for my job. After one year, our total carbon dioxide output is 8.8 tons. That's almost a third of what it used to be.

We used to have no sense of control, but now we have an overview of what's going on in our lives, which makes us much more proactive. We no longer operate in crisis mode. Our *Kanban* board contains a collection of most of our information streams: everything from our budget, school and daycare activities, parties, current events, and weekly menus, to an in-depth, two-week schedule. The puzzle of our life is featured on that board, and the pieces are contained and in place, rather than scattered all over. Our *Kanban* board helps us watch over our streams and plan how we'll meet our needs. Every Sunday, we aim to have a family-wide, fifteen-minute meeting that we call the *Kanban* Meeting. We focus on what's going on in the coming week. We've gone from being reactive to proactive, and for the first time, we can honestly say that we know what's going on. We also try to plan our chores using the *Kanban* board, and we distribute tasks evenly.

In early summer 2011, Mattias did about 75–80% of unpaid housework, and he worked 36 hours a week. I worked 60 hours a week including overtime, and accounted for about 20% of the housework. The kids did almost nothing at all. Today, we both work 40 hours a week, and we share unpaid housework just about equally: around 45% each, while the kids account for around 10%.

Chickens and a Japanese garden

We no longer pay a surcharge for our home, because we've cleared out many unnecessary things that took up space (however, we have quite a few trips left to the recycling bins and charity shops). Before implementing lean at home, we wasted more than 35 square meters of living space with clutter and rooms used for storage. Given the average price of $5,370 per square meter, we paid a surcharge of over $150,000 for our house including utilities. Pure waste. Remember that living space is probably the most expensive thing you've invested in – whether you rent or have a mortgage – and it is a wise principle indeed to only keep the things you love or use daily. Keeping this in mind makes it a bit easier when you come to donate or sell things that you no longer use.

Suddenly, we can get things done, and lean and *Kaizen* (continuous improvements) were catalysts. Where we used to only see problems, we now see opportunities in disguise. Rather than build a pricey paved garage entry in a weed-infested area of our garden, we planted a fledgling Japanese garden. We sanded, repainted, and installed a beautiful piece of stained glass in our unsightly front door, and we didn't have to buy a new one (we also contributed to growth by tasking a skilled glass artist with the job). Our mantra is: if we can buy it used or renovate it, we will give it a try – (we still contribute to the economy by depending on crafts-people).We have many examples of easy improvements we've chosen to make in place of expensive renovations or buying new things. We're saving for pets that also come with benefits: in the garden, we're going to have chickens that will give us eggs we can eat in good conscience, and that we can feed our vegetable peels. We're going to make a small, simple spa in the basement bathroom. In our little spa, we're going to have garra rufa fish, which will give us fish pedicures.

Where had we been?

If we hadn't made these changes, it's likely that I would have gone on sick leave for burnout, and our home would have been impacted by that trauma. Mattias probably wouldn't have resigned from the medical center where economic indicators had surpassed patient safety in importance.

The picture we have now is entirely different. That middle-aged, slightly graying couple looks happier and much more excited today. Our steps are no longer heavy with exhaustion; they have a spring and a bounce to them. I turned in my high heels for bright pink Doc Martens, and that painstak-ingly bleached blonde hair has been changed to strawberry blonde.

A year after we had introduced lean into our home Mattias decided to resign from the medical center that only focused on financial indi-cators. He works full-time today while I've gone from working 60 hours a week to a more standard 40 hours, and I'm achieving my dream of writing a trilogy.

So if we were to invite a Toyota leader over to our home, someone who has worked with lean for decades, what would he say if we asked, is our home lean?

I believe he would look at us a little sadly, as if we were missing some-thing, and say, "I don't know. I wasn't here when you started introduc-ing lean."

Because lean isn't a goal in and of itself. It's a means to achieve what you want, to create the home you want, and to fulfill the dreams you and your loved ones share. Lean is dynamic. Lean prevents stagna-tion, going backwards, freezing up, rather than continuously evolv-ing. Just like life itself, you are never done.

What have we achieved in our home in just over a year of lean at home?

Streams – from bottlenecks to smoothness and flow

- Our laundry stream is ten times faster than it was.

- Our clothes are washed and ironed, and our shoes are in good condition when we need them.

- We've reduced our clothing and shoe costs from $700 per month to $120.

- We no longer have some twenty piles of clothes around the house, taking up a total floor space worth around $53,670.

- Our information overload is under control. We keep track of all information that requires any kind of decision, payment, or filing.

- We have a budget stream in which we work together to plan purchases, and we've cut our spending in half.

- We reuse and recycle everything we possibly can, and the kids are involved.

- The barriers and bottlenecks that prevented us from getting things done are largely gone. Suddenly, things happen.

- Generally speaking, our days run much more smoothly than they used to, and we even achieve a sense of flow.

Kaizen – continuous improvements

- Rather than seeing problems everywhere, we see our home with fresh eyes that are more accepting and less judgmental.

- With *Kaizen* as our catalyst, we have started making many small changes. We make sure to finish what we start.

- We have also made several major improvements to things that used to cause irritation.

- All the living space that once served as collection and sorting areas has been freed up.

Muda – stop wasting

- We save at least $4,600 per year simply by bringing a packed lunch.

- We throw away very little food, and our meals are planned, seasonal, and locally sourced.

- Our total energy costs today are one-third of what they were, thanks to the improvements we've made since starting lean at home.

- Before, our joint annual carbon dioxide emissions totaled 25.8 tons. If everyone lived like us, we would need more than eight planets. Today, we've reduced our annual emissions to 8.8 tons of carbon dioxide.

- Instead of spending an average of 700 minutes a week searching for things, the total time all five of us spend searching is just 70 minutes a week.

- Today, we can usually recognize when we are doing extra work right away – because remember, the awful thing about extra work is that you often think you're doing something value-creating.

Kanban – visual planning

- We made a lean at home *Kanban* board that contains the puzzle pieces that form our life.

- We try to have a fifteen-minute meeting every Sunday, where our entire family focuses on what the upcoming week holds. For the first time ever, we can say things are under control.

- We schedule chores and make sure we have time to rest.

- We know when each upcoming celebration will be, and we can do something fun for everything from International Women's Day to Ramadan. We no longer miss birthdays.

- The *Kanban* board has improved our ability to sync with others, which lets us help out with carpooling and more.

- We learned how to synchronize the calendars on our phones, giving us simultaneous, automatic access to everyone's schedules.

Seiri – sort and purge

- Before, we paid a surcharge of around $150,000 for our home, considering how we used it.

- There was always at least one room that was unusable, because we stored so much stuff there (at any given time, it could have been the dressing room, workroom, or playroom in the basement).

- We have created a variation of the 5S program (sorting, setting in order, systematic cleaning, standardizing, and sustaining). It is a sacred tradition, and we call it Clean-o-rama.

- Everything in its place: we bought small white labels (1 cm x 4 cm) and put them on boxes and cabinets to help us remember what goes where. We've shed the counterproductive collisions of dancing around one another's solutions.

Hansei – reflection, learning

- In spring 2011, I was on the brink of sick leave for burnout, and we were at a crossroads.

- After neglecting exercise for the last ten years, Mattias is running a marathon, and I'm training for a triathlon and Tjejklassikern, the women's classic circuit.

- The kids are realizing their dreams to a greater extent (although I've promised not to write what they are…).

- Mattias quit working at the medical center that emphasized economic indicators over quality, and started at a clinic that focuses on patients.

- I'm on my way to achieving a dream I've had since I was a child: writing a trilogy, which I'm about to complete.

- Instead of being annoyed at one another's spending habits, which culminated in once-monthly arguments, we have a budget and we discuss our purchases.

- We've formed agreements about how to do various things, and we're trying to stick to them. And that's key: sitting down, talking about what's important, what you value most – and respecting each other's values.

- By following up what we've done, our changes and the routines we've agreed upon are lasting.

Mura and *Muri* – leaving overloads and uneven streams behind

- In early summer 2011, Mattias accounted for almost 75–80% of unpaid housework, and he worked 36 hours a week. I worked 60 hours a week including overtime, and accounted for about 20% of the housework.

- Today, we both work 40 hours a week, and we share unpaid housework just about equally: around 45% each.

- Our children are more involved and contribute on their terms; they're responsible for about 10% of the housework. That number will increase gradually as they get older.

- We are much better at acknowledging one another's efforts.

- Using the visual management of our *Kanban* board, we're learning to be much better at planning, and at dividing up the housework evenly. This way, everything doesn't happen at once.

13

LEAN AT HOME
AT YOUR PLACE

I recently spoke with an unusually wise man, Sven, who has been a Toyota plant manager for decades. We were in an Executive MBA program at the Stockholm School of Economics together. His mission is to inspire subcontractors to implement lean, and this is his mantra: "Do not do everything at once. One thing at a time. Begin with visualization, and take control of a process that is important for you to change and have run smoothly. Think of long- and short-term goals."

If you're starting to implement lean at home, then that is my message to you as well. Take it step-by-step. You have oceans of time ahead of you if you want to work sustainably with lean at home. Start by visualizing and have a *Kanban* Meeting with your family. There's so much to gain from making everything that forms your family stream visible. Everyone will share the same picture of what's going on, how it's happening, and even what isn't happening. That makes it harder to shirk responsibility; everything is clear, visible. In addition, you'll stop living parallel lives with no insight into what's happening around you. You will lay the foundation for going from zero control to total control.

After visualizing, sit down together to consider a stream you want to change. Choose one that offers a great deal to gain from making improvements. Get the stream under control and determine what is value-creating and what is pure waste. Think of how you can reduce waste and improve stream efficiency, one way at a time. Create the conditions for flow.

At the same time, you can start talking about what you consider a good home and what you do not, if you haven't already done this at some point. Because if lean at home is about how to create the life you live together at home, then you need to know just what kind of life you want to live.

To be sure, lean is a coherent strategy and philosophy based on sustainability, participation, and respect for fellow beings and the environment. But that doesn't mean you have to do everything at once. To truly reap the rewards of implementing lean at home, think long-term: avoid hailstorms of creativity and activity that quickly melt away to reveal the return of the status quo. Lean at home is a strategy, a tool for those of us who don't naturally have a knack for organization in our daily lives. What was once a burden can be enriching.

Here are a few of the most essential principles for implementing lean at home. Consider what will be the most valuable for you. No system is right for everyone, so see this as a smorgasbord and choose the things that are important to you in your life. And remember: you do not have to do everything. The most important part is beginning.

- *Go from frustration to smoothness and flow.* Review the most important streams in your home. Remember, a stream is that which takes place from the time a need arises until it is satisfied. Toyoda saw streams metaphorically as threads: where does the thread begin, where does it end, and what happens in between? What causes frustration and bottlenecks? Which streams will be most beneficial to change? Start there. How much of what you do creates value? Calculate your stream efficiency. For example, how does your food stream look, from buying groceries to handling dishes and leftovers after a meal?

- *When you consider your home as a huge needs factory, can you tell which and whose needs you prioritize?* Ask yourself if they are important, fundamental needs, or if they tend to be compensatory needs. One way to test yourselves is by reviewing Maslow's hierarchy of needs. Do you meet everyone's basic needs, giving all members of your family the chance to achieve self-actualization? Far too often, we fail to meet basic needs and spend tons of resources on compensatory needs instead, which is downright wasteful. Perhaps worst of all, we prioritize our most important needs last – sleep, exercise, healthy food, clean air and water, socializing with friends – to satisfy needs we didn't even realize we had until confronted with an onslaught of advertisements. In order to truly benefit from lean at home, it is essential to devote your energy and intentions to genuinely important and valuable streams.

- *Waste less time and money; lighten your load on the environment.* Review where and why you have waste. Ask the question why five times, and you'll find the reason, not just the symptoms. How can you reduce or completely eliminate waste? Continuously striving to reduce all forms of waste is a cornerstone of lean. Every home may have unique challenges, but one dilemma is common to most: we have an enormous number of needs combined with a real or perceived lack of time, money, and resources. Reducing waste allows us to focus on and tend to the things we truly value and deem important. We are hard on one another's love, trust and self-esteem; we are hard on the environment and we waste our money. Lean at home dramatically reduces waste.

- *Try seeing problems and challenges as opportunities in disguise to create a culture of continuous improvements.* Seeing issues as opportunities to improve can bring about a change in perspective. You will be less judgmental and more accepting. Practice *Kaizen*, and be sure to start making changes that same week. Lean is about implementation, putting into action, trial and error. Remember how things were before you began working with lean at home by taking pictures of piles of clothes, analysing costs, and timing how long various processes take. Analysis is important to create new, improved procedures. Start from your current situation when sketching out how you want your future to be. After you've analysed how things are and why, it will be easier to establish the right conditions and procedures to achieve your desired scenario. We're not talking about ongoing, expensive renovation projects. Instead, think in terms of taking lots of small steps to organize your home and create a family life with space for all members to grow.

- *Reflect on how you want your home to be.* Contemplate what is important to your home and daily life. What are your goals? How can your home contribute to your family's goals and the needs of each member? Should it be a safe home base to rest? An energetic environment? An open, welcoming home for socializing? Lean at home isn't a goal in and of itself; it's a strategy to create the home you want. Make sure you don't stop at daydreams and an attempt to escape reality: realize your dreams, and create smoothness. Your goals should be clear, attractive, and possible to realize. They shouldn't feel like rules. It's important for each family member to contribute his or her perspective. Think of your home as a fragile, newly planted tree: how can you help it grow stronger and more beautiful?

- *Review your current follow-up method.* Monitoring, evaluating, and self-reflection are pillars of lean. Ongoing evaluation and reflection – *Hansei* – are ways to replace your silent, solo evaluation with a dialogue. Work together to make sure you are traveling down the same path, and to make sure that path is taking you the right way. Create a dialogue – not a confrontation – where you can meet and discuss whether you're on the right track. In lean, mistakes are seen as a chance to learn. Lean at home will help your family and your home become a center of learning instead of consumption – and isn't that what we want?

- *Implement visual planning and management,* called *Kanban*, which will give you a shared "air-traffic control center" and motivate you to be more proactive, enabling you to assemble all of the pieces of your life into a single picture. This is a place for the whole family to share the same information about what's going on. It's about taking joint ownership of events, preventing responsibility from resting solely on one parent's increasingly burdened shoulders. If you are the home's informal, unpaid project leader, resign immediately. With clear, joint planning that is updated daily, and a once-weekly, fifteen-minute *Kanban* Meeting, everyone will share the same information. Make decisions about who does what to prevent things from slipping between the cracks, and to escape the constant anxiety that you've forgotten something important. Clear, evident planning creates predictability and expectation: you can plan, you can dream, you can take charge.

- *Review participation: how do you distribute chores so that no one is overloaded?* What kind of informal contract do you have at home? Try the following exercise: sit down with a sheet of white paper in front of each of you, and draw a column indicating how much housework you do. Write down precisely what you do, from washing the car to making birthday party invitations. Include absolutely everything. Make another column illustrating your perception of what your partner does. If you do this exercise with an open mind and a bit of self-insight, the work often amounts to more than you might think. And if your kids are old enough, make a column for them, too. If they can write, they can also participate in the exercise by writing down what they do. If you understand what other people contribute, it will be easier to appreciate their efforts. Once you've done this exercise, it may also be a good time to revise your gender contract a bit.

- *Use 5S to create order and tidiness.* Room by room, consider what function each room serves, what things are necessary for the room to meet that function, and what things you enjoy seeing. Use the five Ss: *Seiri* – sort out seldom used items, *Seiton* – establish structure, so that everything has a place, *Seiso* – shine up and clean out, *Seiketsu* – standardize and create rules to make your efforts last, and *Shitsuke* – sustain by creating a habit. Find inspiration in Clean-o-rama, which could be as much of an institution in your home as it is in ours.

- *Remember, you may suffer from setbacks*, as with all changes. It would be strange if you didn't. But don't let that become a reason to stop working on changes. Doubt, confusion and resistance are inherent components of change. Return to what you wanted to change and why. Also, reflect on the following:

- *Remember your dreams:* what did you dream when you first met your partner? What did you dream when you locked eyes with your children for the first time? What did you want to give, and what did you hope to receive? Set up pictures of your dreams; distinguish between daydreams and what you can plan and carry out. Differentiate between actual needs, and needs someone else tries to make you believe you have. Think about how many sick people struggle to return to everyday life. Instead of trying to escape the daily grind, make a serious effort to create flow in your life. Let that be your reality.

14

GETTING STARTED – EASY TIPS

As I said earlier, our initial efforts to introduce lean at home were unconscious; it was pure survival instinct. Once we saw the pattern, we started to systematically and intentionally implement lean at home. We reviewed the various pillars of lean, and gradually, we introduced them in our home. But as I've written many times before: you don't have to do it all at once. You don't even have to do it all in one lifetime. But you do have to get going and do something. You may know exactly how to get started now. In that case, stop reading here and begin. These last lines are meant for those of you who want to start, but don't quite know where. To eliminate what is hopefully the last bottleneck, I'll finish with some incredibly practical, hands-on advice for how to begin.

Buy a whiteboard and narrow black tape, and tape horizontal and vertical lines to form a table. Horizontally, you'll have one row for each family member, one row for celebrations, one for meal planning and one for chores. Vertically, you'll have 14 columns, which is a two-week period. Once you have your table drawn, use a whiteboard pen to write each family member's name and the days of the week. Then, list every single activity coming up in the next two weeks. Decide the week's menu; decide when certain chores will be done, and see if any celebrations are coming up, anything from a birthday to Independence Day. Have your first *Kanban* Meeting with the entire family.

Stand in front of the board and spend fifteen minutes max on the meeting.

If you can't choose which stream to begin with, start either with food, recycling, or clothing. Choose whichever would benefit the most from a change.

Calculate your environmental footprint. Visit the World Wildlife Fund's (WWF) website or Global Footprint Network (where you measure what you treasure). Calculate how many planets would be necessary if everyone lived as your household does. Set an attainable goal for how much you can reduce your footprint; discuss how to do it.

Attach a sheet of white paper to the refrigerator. Make two columns. Label one STOP DOING. Label one TO SELL/DONATE. Write down everything you will stop doing, from sitting in front of the TV when the kids have gone to bed, to manically cleaning the kitchen cabinets. Decide what to sell or give away – everything from a picture you don't think is worth anything that you've never liked, to your kids' old shoes in the basement.

Start having a Clean-o-rama. Pick one day each week for the whole family to clean the house, and think of a fun way to celebrate when you're done. It may help to make a pretty "Clean-o-rama is in progress" sign, as well as signs listing procedures for each room. After Clean-o-rama, the kids get to inspect your efforts, and their own, to make sure everything has been thoroughly cleaned. Celebrate when you finish.

When you chose to open this book, you had a need. I sincerely hope it has met your expectations, and that now you can make the changes you need in your unique life. The real journey begins today: embrace it with curiosity in the here and now.

Author's Acknowledgments

In my wildest dreams, I never would have imagined that writing a book like this would take so much time. So many people have contributed in various ways. Without you, it would still exist only in my computer. Without your relentless encouragement, I never would have taken the next step – because it is indeed a mighty task for a naturally private person such as myself to write this kind of book.

First and foremost, five people created the content of this book, even if I'm the one who sat behind the keyboard. So Mattias, Vendela, Tuva and Samuel are absolutely co-authors.

My parents, big brother, and sister-in-law Joanna always offered smart opinions and advice. A crowd of friends passed through all the security gates to read the manuscript and give their various perspectives – Mona, Per, Marie, Stina, Micke, Maria, Ingrid, Åsa and Kia.

Peter and Sven, who read the manuscript with a sound knowledge of lean, and gave their essential blessing along the way.

My writing coach, Ann Ljungberg, because when I was ready to throw in the towel, you believed in my manuscript. My wonderful agent, Jennifer Thompson at Nordlyset Agency, and Tamsin English and Natalie Bradley at Yellow Kite, for putting so much love into the book. And for the English edition, my fantastic translator Amanda Larsson, who carefully and pitch-perfectly translated the original Swedish text into English.

Last but not least, my Aunt Biggan, because she was a true everyday heroine.

THANK YOU

books to help you live a good life

Join the conversation and tell
us how you live a #goodlife

🐦 @yellowkitebooks
f YellowKiteBooks
𝒫 Yellow Kite Books
📷 YellowKiteBooks